Our Keepsakes

OUR KEEPSAKES: A Picture Book of Keepsakes, Treasures, and Memories.
Copyright © 2019 by James E. Gilliam. All rights reserved.

ISBN: 9781072848257

Our Keepsakes:

A Picture Book of Keepsakes, Treasures, and Mementos

Residents of Longhorn Village
share objects
they hold on to and cherish

Jim Gilliam

Introduction

Over our lifetime, we have collected many things. All special, but some are more special than others; they are keepsakes. Most of us have at least one object that we hold dear. These objects have special meaning and they speak to our past, and we don't want to let go of them. They often tell remarkable stories about our sentiments, values, and life experiences. Their stories need to be shared.

This book gives a glimpse at the fascinating collection of personal treasures of the residents of Longhorn Village, a retirement community in Austin, Texas. Stories and photos include items about Buffalo Bill Cody's bridle bit, an IOU from Jim Bowie, the last portrait of Abraham Lincoln, an Astronaut's patch from the Challenger disaster, objects of love, historical artifacts, and other unique personal objects. Each has a story. Told in their own words, the people share their thoughts and sentiments about their keepsakes.

This book is different from other books I've written. First of all, it's a picture book; my other books have been either texts or psychological tests. Second, this book is based on contributors' writings or a summary of my interviews with the contributors; my other publications have been more scholarly in nature. Third, for me, writing is hard work; but this book was fun to write because the keepsakes told the story. Fourth, all royalties from sales of this book go to the Longhorn Village Residents' Foundation to aid residents with financial needs.

Most people who have talked with me about this book are complimentary. They think the topic is interesting; that people who contributed to the book probably had a lot of interesting stuff; and it must have been fun talking to people about their keepsakes. I'm often asked, "How did you come up with the idea for the book? My answer is, "Milt caused it to happen."

My friend, Milt Simpson, is a prolific, creative author of many books about unusual, quirky, esoteric subjects. A few of his book titles are: **Windmill Weights** (Johnson & Simpson), **Folk Erotica** (Harper Collins), and **The Visual Memoir** (Blurb.com). He publishes at least one book a year. Milt asked me to help him with a photo book he wanted to do about business cards.

Shortly after we started on the book, Milt fell and was hospitalized for a couple of weeks. During hospital visits we talked about his book and the more we talked, the more I became disenchanted with the business card topic. But talking with him got me thinking about the unusual things Milt collects; for example, chopstick rests, yo-yo's, kitchen timers, musical spoons, and other esoteric objects. The more I thought about Milt's collections, I began to think about things I have saved. And that got me thinking about what other people collect and save. I concluded that probably everyone saves things; and some are keepsakes. And that's how I came up with the idea for this book. I thought, "Wouldn't it be interesting to do a book on keepsakes?" That's how the idea came to me. So, if Milt hadn't fallen, this book probably wouldn't have happened. Thank you Milt.

Before I talk about the keepsakes that are featured in this book, I will tell you a little about Longhorn Village where Milt and I and all the contributors to this book live. Longhorn Village is a retirement community in Austin, Texas. Approximately 300 remarkable people live there. They come from all over the United States, are highly educated, have fascinating backgrounds and experiences, and had remarkable careers in a variety of occupations. Each person has a unique and interesting story, and their keepsakes are informative about them.

Because their keepsakes and stories are unique, there was no easy way to group them into chapters--thus, no table of contents. I decided to organize the book alphabetically according to the keepsake owner's last name. Depending on whether a story took one or two pages, I made exceptions with alphabetizing to make things fit. You will find each contributor's name in the index in the back of the book. On occasion when there was a blank page, I included photos of events, activities, or other topics that provide a glimpse of Longhorn Village and the people who live there.

    The stories in the book were either written by the individual whose keepsake is presented or were written by me after I interviewed them about their keepsake. All stories and photographs were approved by the contributor before they were included in the book. With few exceptions, the photographs were taken by me.

    I hope you like the book and I hope you will say, "What a neat idea; how interesting. I never thought about a book on keepsakes." Who knows, maybe it will inspire you to do a book on something you find interesting.

The Keepsakes and Their Stories

My Nilavilakku
Sany Abraham

My keepsake is the Nilavilakku made by my brother. First I will tell you about the Nilavilakku. It is a traditional lamp used commonly in Kerala, and other parts of India. *Nilam* in the Malayalam/Tamil language means floor or the ground and *vilakku* means lamp.

These traditional lamps are lit during auspicious occasions; in temples before the worship starts; at official and unofficial functions, and they are commonly lit as a ritual in many households. They are also used in art forms such as dances and plays. The Nilavilakku is usually made of bronze or brass, but is sometimes made of other materials. Usually cotton wicks doused in oil or ghee are used for lighting the lamp. There are three ways of lighting the lamp. In one, only one wick is lit and is directed towards the deity or sacred space and in another there are two lit wicks in two directions. The third alternative is with five wicks in five directions.

My Nilavilakku is special to me for many reasons. It was made for me by my baby brother in 1965. It is completely hand-made and is comprised of rice grains. The grains were laboriously sewn together and then glued to a wooden base that forms the lamp. My brother gave the Nilavilakku to us as a special gift as we were leaving for the United States. He passed away three years ago, so the Nilavilakku has special meaning as it reminds me of my brother and what he meant to me and my family. It also reminds me of my former home and culture. It is a wonderful keepsake.

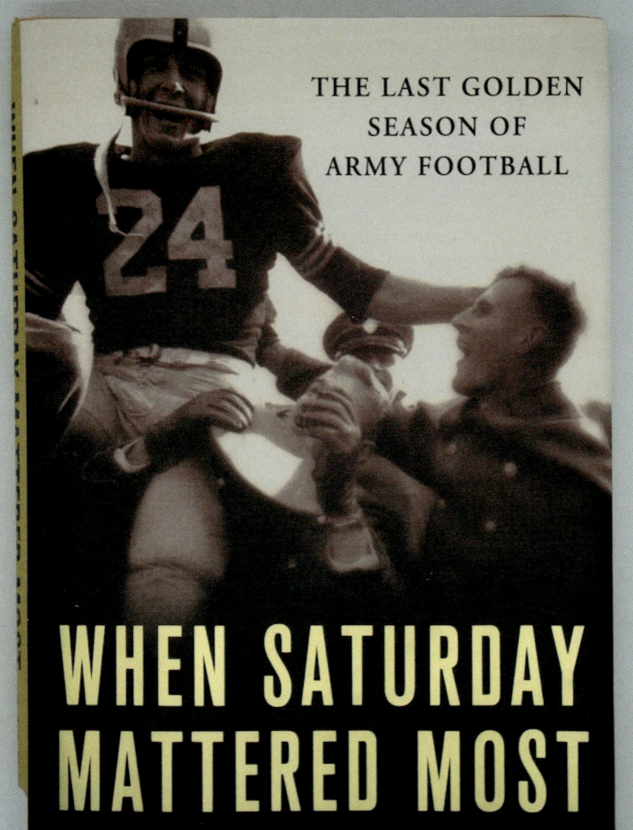

THE LAST GOLDEN SEASON OF ARMY FOOTBALL

WHEN SATURDAY MATTERED MOST

"A special season, never to be repeated."
—LEIGH MONTVILLE, *New York Times* bestselling author

MARK BEECH

The Last Golden Season of Army Football
Glen Adams

My keepsake is the book, ***When Saturday Mattered Most*** by Mark Beech who was a West Point graduate and a staff writer at *Sports Illustrated*. The book is special to me because it tells the story of an historic year in Army football. But more than that, it tells stories about my friends, teammates, coaches, army brass, and all that went into that remarkable season. I am proud to have been a part of that team and what we accomplished.

I was fortunate to receive an appointment to the United States Military Academy in 1957. I have always felt that I was lucky and my entry into the storied football program at West Point was an example. I grew up in El Paso, Texas and went to Ysleta High School. I was a pretty good football player and during my junior year, General Terry de la Mesa-Allen saw me play. He went to my principal and asked about me, particularly how I was as a student. Specifically, he wanted to know about my grades. Once satisfied that I might be able to compete academically, he recommended me to Coach Earl "Red" Blaik.

In those days, freshmen were not allowed to play varsity football, so I did not get into any games. But the next year, 1958, I was lucky enough to play and even start on defense. Blaik entered the 1958 season as the longest tenured coach in college football and he built a team that was outstanding. It included a Heisman Trophy winner, Pete Dawkins, and seven All-Americans (but I wasn't one of them). We ended the season undefeated and ranked third in the nation. If you like football, I think you will like the book.

Grandmothers' Paperweights
Kay Allison

The most difficult part of participating in this special project is choosing what keepsake to share. Almost everything I moved to my apartment is a keepsake to me - furniture, paintings, books, small items - the list goes on and on. And, I have added my own "keepsakes" from my life and various trips that I hope will be meaningful to my children and grandchildren someday. These treasures bring me such joy when I see them and remind me of family and friends that have been so important in my life. I love that I can reach out and touch something used or admired by those who have gone before.

I finally chose my mother's paperweight collection. She thoughtfully distributed a few of her favorites at the end of her life - a bit like sharing what she loved with those she loved. She collected these paperweights throughout her life - a few old ones came from her family, some came from her limited travels, but most came from her children and friends who brought gifts we all knew she would appreciate. She displayed most of her collection on a round coffee table in her living room. I am grateful to have a few from her collection and enjoy them as she did - their beauty, their differences, their expression of thoughtfulness of others, and, yes, their occasional usefulness in holding down those pieces of paper that want to fly off a desk!

What I love best about choosing my collection of paperweights as my keepsake is the ease of sharing it. The decision of who should get a treasured item is eliminated because everyone will get a keepsake from my collection. Memories stay alive when shared, and when a child or grandchild asks about a particular keepsake, the perfect opportunity arises to tell the story about their grandmothers, and that is a joy.

Diamond Engagement Ring
Peggy Appleby

My keepsake is a platinum cocktail ring which I designed and had a jeweler create to hold the diamonds from my mother's engagement and wedding band.

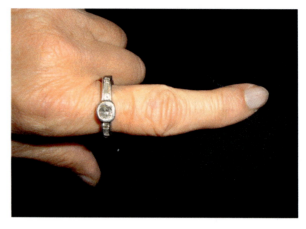

She wanted me to have these rings, but she wore them every day until she passed away in 2005. The rings, when I inherited them, were not in very good condition. The diamonds were loose and the center diamond looked as if it was about to fall out of the setting. With safety as my primary concern, I designed a cocktail ring which would hold the center one-carat diamond and have baguettes and round diamonds on each side of the center stone. I had a jeweler cast my design into a heavy platinum ring and he set the diamonds deeply into the setting.

I wear this ring 24 hours a day, 7 days a week, and think of my mom every time I look at it. She would be very happy with the ring and especially grateful for my concern about keeping her diamonds safe. I am proud of my ability to design a beautiful ring and I am very happy with my mom's diamonds. I feel as if my mom and I planned this together even though she passed away 14 years ago.

Aviator's Watch of the Greatest Generation

Chuck Armitage

My keepsake is a watch that was given to me by a good friend of mine, John Klauck. I met John in Sarasota, Florida in 1970. He was a well-respected businessman and I was just starting out in a retail souvenir shop. We became close friends and he and I and our wives traveled all over the world together. I collected watches and when John learned of this, he gave me this tarnished, old watch. Its significance is that it is the watch that John wore in World War II when he was flying B-17s in Sarasota. He was a mentor to me and one of the "greatest generation." Today, it is old and tarnished but it still keeps perfect time. It reminds me of him and what a great guy he was.

Baba's Diary
Sue Bartosh

My ancestors emigrated from Ireland around 1850 and settled in Northern California - around Susanville. They were farmers and merchants and their families grew and prospered. My father was born in 1905. He was a rancher and had a John Deere/Caterpillar dealership in Susanville. My mother was a homemaker and never went far from home because she never learned to drive. My father and mother lived their entire lives in this same area and never traveled far from home.

In the 1970's, my husband Ray and I lived in Hong Kong where he worked for Dow Chemical company. We decided that my parents should come and visit us there. It was a major step for them to travel at all and a giant leap for them to travel such a distance and to a foreign country. After much planning, they decided to make the trip. The local newspaper took up their story and started writing articles about the "Big Trip" for a local couple. Each morning my father met with his buddies at the local coffee shop and updated everyone on the plans. The whole community was caught up in this adventure for two of their own. They seemed to vicariously experience my parents' trip.

The trip turned out to be everything they could have expected. My son gave my father a journal before the trip so he could describe details of their experience. And describe details he did! He filled 109 pages with details; recording dates, times, where they ate, what they ate, what they did, who they did things with, and other observations. It was and still is a true treasure to read his meticulous notes about their journey and see Hong Kong through his eyes.

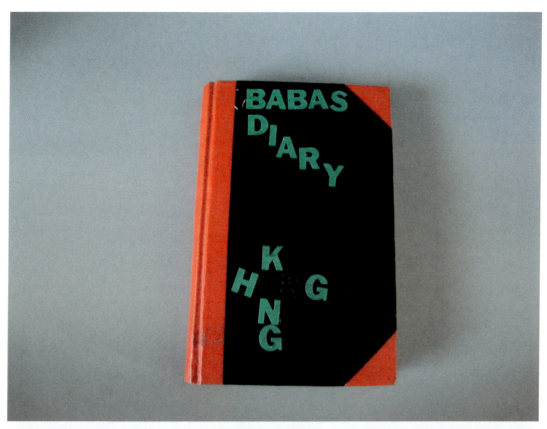

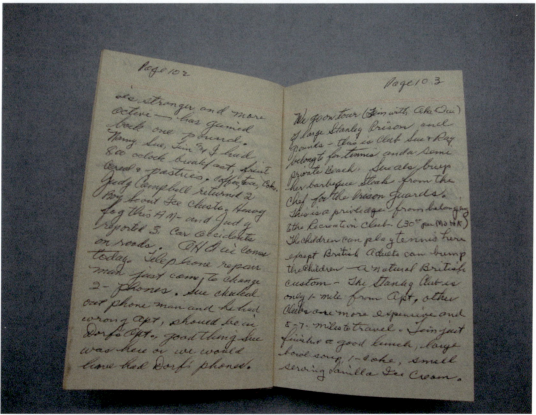

United States Army Air Force Bracelet
Eddy Beckelhymer

My keepsake is a child's bracelet given to me by my half-brother, Earl Hall, in 1940. I believe it was purchased in Hawaii, where he was stationed. It has the wings insignia of the U.S. Army Air Force centered on the links with a ruby on each side. He was a Captain at Hickam Field in Hawaii on December 7, 1941 when Pearl Harbor was attacked. He was a pilot of B-17 bombers and flew missions in the South Pacific until he was shot down and killed on February 1, 1943 in Bougainville. He was posthumously promoted to Major.

Befi's Lamp
Mary and Tony Befi

Our keepsake is a golden lamp that we bought in 1965. We were living in our first home in the Bronx, New York when we purchased it. It was a little pricey for us at the time but we fell in love with it and had to have it for our new home. We also bought a chandelier that matched but we were unable to take it with us when we moved. The lamp has survived our two sons, four grandkids, and one great-grandchild, and all of our moves; so, it is sturdy as well as stunning. People always tell us it is captivating and catches their eye when they enter our apartment. It may not be Aladdin's Lamp but it is definitely Befi's Lamp.

So Many Questions
Wallace and Mary Louise Behrhorst

After all these years___ seventy-six, no less___ Mary Louise and I still wonder about this photograph. We know the year; it was the summer of 1942. We were 15. We know the place;___ Camp Cauble, near Benedict, Kansas. And we know the occasion; the last day of a one-week camp for Lutheran teen-agers. But why? And, what?

The "what?" first. That box…. or case… that "thing"… between us, at our feet. What is it? Whose is it? Seventy-six years later, we wonder. On, perhaps, a more profound level: Why are we sitting together? And that begs the more puzzling question: Why did I keep the picture for all these years? Sure, we first met at the camp and for one week, we did all those things that kids do at a church camp. We became acquainted; friends that is. Even, maybe, good friends. But more than 100 teen-agers attended that camp. So, why wasn't someone else (besides Mary Louise and me) in the picture? And what about the "box" between us? What did it all mean?

These questions surfaced many, many, years after the event itself. Interestingly, for two years we attended the same high school, St. John's Academy in Winfield, Kansas, and for a year and a half, went to Saint John's College together. We were good friends still, and we ran with the same crowd on campus. But that was about it; never dated, etc. I graduated and transferred to Concordia Seminary in St. Louis, studying to be a Lutheran pastor (which I became in 1950). Mary Louise graduated and transferred to Valparaiso University, studied voice, got married in 1947 (to a pastor whom I had known in college as a classmate of my older brother who also attended

St. John's). After graduating from the Seminary, I got married. Mary Louise went her way; I mine. Over the years, many of them, we saw one another at church conventions, school class reunions, etc. On those chance meetings, we reconnected as friends with separate lives.

The years passed. Lots of water "spilled over the dam," as the saying goes. In time, thanks to one of her daughters, we reconnected (and how that happened is another story). That was June 2016. To make a long story short, over the next few months, I wrote her, she wrote me; I called her; she called me; I visited her; she visited me. We traveled here and there, getting better acquainted again. And on April 12, 2017, we said our "I do's." Both of us were in our 90's, seventy years after that photo was taken.

We are profoundly grateful that our lives have come together again. Still, the questions remain about the picture. Why was it taken? And why did I keep it? Why didn't it go the way of the hundreds of other pictures taken___ tossed away when distances and chains of events separate. And, most curiously: What is that "box" situated between us? We may never know. But searching for answers will, no doubt, be the subject for pillow-talk on many nights in our future.

My Special Heart-Shaped Stone
Marc Bernat

Placing a stone on the tombstone of a friend or loved one is a Jewish practice that goes back at least to early medieval times. Numerous claims have been made as to the significance and reasons why. Placing a rock on the tombstone or grave honors the deceased and lets others know that the deceased is being visited. Putting stones on the grave is also believed to keep the deceased's soul near the grave for a few moments longer, which is comforting to the loved ones. While any stone will do, one often seeks a stone that seems different or special.

Gravel from the parking lot at the cemetery is a common source of rocks, but sometimes people bring a special rock to the service. My efforts have always been to seek a stone with a little personality or different shape.

On the occasion of my Mother's burial, I located an appropriate gravel rock. As I picked it up, my eyes were drawn to an adjacent rock. I picked up both. The adjacent rock is my keepsake. It is sort of shaped like a heart. I felt my Mother convey her wish that I keep it. So, I put the first rock on the tombstone, and I kept my keepsake. Wherever I travel, my keepsake and my Mother go with me.

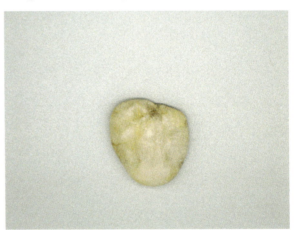

A Keepsake from My Honeymoon
Sharon Bishop

My late husband, Bill, and I met when I was 28 and he was 30. After a 6-month courtship, we had a small wedding and reception in 1965. Since both of us had jobs with a lot of responsibility, there was time for only a four-day honeymoon at the World's Fair in New York City. Bill made reservations at the Americana, a fairly upscale hotel at that time. I waited in the lobby while he checked us in. After about 15 minutes he grabbed me with one hand and our bags with the other and said, "We're leaving!" The Americana had given away our reservations but arranged for us to stay at the Drake hotel, nearby. It was a nice hotel but not as fancy as the Americana. Bill fumed, but I thought it was kind of funny and something memorable. As a souvenir, I snitched this ashtray. Now this ashtray, my keepsake, makes me smile and brings back memories of the great time we had.

Cherry Wood Pipe
Jim Bissett

This pipe was made in one piece from the trunk and branch of a cherry tree. The hole in the stem was made with a hot wire. I smoked it a few times years ago and it performed well and gave a pleasant taste to the tobacco.

The maker was my grandfather, John Kyle Bissett, who died of the flu in 1920 when my father was only 10 years old. My father barely remembered him. It is an interesting keepsake and is the only memento I have of him.

A Sailing I Shall Go
Jim Blauvelt

From my early teens, I was interested in boats and navigation. My father was also interested in sailing and navigation. He had a copy of *The American Practical Navigator,* usually referred to as the *Bowditch,* which is an encyclopedia of navigation. It serves as a valuable oceanography and meteorology handbook, and contains useful tables and a maritime glossary. I used to read it and study its tables.

For many years after college, I was involved in small class sailboat racing along the East coast and I competed in the competitions for the 1960 United States Olympic team in the Flying Dutchman class. We didn't win but it was a great experience. I also crewed and skippered on many larger boats in other contests.

I always wanted to do a real ocean voyage as the navigator using the traditional method of a sextant rather than the new electronic aided systems. So, I was delighted to be asked to skipper, and navigate a 40-foot sailboat competing in the 1978 Newport to Bermuda race. My keepsakes are memorabilia from that race.

Aunt Grace's Earrings
Edna Bocek

While I retain no memory of having met my Aunt Grace, she has always been my favorite aunt. A couple of months after I was born, Aunt Grace died of tuberculosis in a Phoenix sanitarium. Knowing that her life was nearing its end, Aunt Grace begged my mother to bring me to Phoenix so she could meet me. So, Mom and I, her infant daughter, boarded a train in Southeastern Missouri, destination Arizona. Unfortunately, my mother related no details of the meeting. I was born in November; Aunt Grace died the following February.

As I grew up, Aunt Grace's picture remained on Mom's bedroom dresser. Her beautiful, kind face made me long to know the woman who died so young. I took it as a compliment when my mother, in moments of pique, shook her head and said, "You're just like your Aunt Grace." While the two of them shared a close relationship, their personalities differed greatly. My feisty mother was quick to laugh and quick to anger. She grew up as a tomboy with a strong dislike for sewing and reading. Aunt Grace, however, as portrayed in Mom's stories of her, approached life with a patient, contemplative attitude. And she crocheted and embroidered beautifully, doing so for hours at a time. My mother keenly felt her sister's passing, and her stories painted a portrait of Aunt Grace that came alive for me.

My keepsakes from Aunt Grace include a few pictures and this pair of ruby earrings. Though our lives overlapped a mere two or three months, I look forward to meeting Aunt Grace again in heaven.

A keepsake is an object retained in memory of something or someone; kept for sentimental or nostalgic reasons.

My Keepsake
James Boldebuck

My treasured keepsake is a hand-cranked wall mounted telephone that I believe to be at least 100 years old. It is special to me for a couple of reasons. It belonged to my grandparents and it was the first telephone that I talked on.

I was born in Comanche County, Texas in 1933. At that time, all parts of the county did not have electrical power or telephone lines. My grandparents lived in a different county that did have telephone lines but not electrical power. It was a big thing for me to occasionally be allowed to briefly talk on their telephone.

You did not have a phone number in those days. Each subscriber was assigned a number of rings. I still remember my grandparents' ring was Two Longs and One Short. Of course, you could eavesdrop on everyone's conversations because each time you cranked the phone, it rang on all phones on the line.

Their telephone was mounted next to the fireplace mantle. Since I was only 4 or 5 years old at the time, I couldn't reach the telephone. I remember in order to speak in the mouthpiece, I had to stand on a box which was used to store wood for the fireplace.

This telephone is not only a fond memory of my childhood but also a reminder of how far we have come with technology in 85 years!

Mamaw's Watch
Wanda Boldebuck

Even though this lady's pocket watch may not be worth a lot of money, I will always treasure it because it belonged to my Grandmother "Mamaw." The watch was given to her in 1905 by her then fiancé, aka as my "Papaw". It is dainty and feminine with love birds in rose gold and is engraved with his initials, which I understand was the custom in those days. In their wedding picture (where the husband is seated with the wife standing behind), Mamaw is proudly wearing her new watch pinned to her dress.

Raising 6 children and being of modest means, life was not always easy for Mamaw, but I never knew her to complain. Strong-willed, she was also a jolly person who looked on the bright side of life. She welcomed any and every one into her heart and home and to her table.

She played ragtime piano (by ear), loved to sing and dance and just cut-up in general. I believe she would have loved living at Longhorn Village and Longhorn Village would have loved her.

The watch kept accurate time until a few years ago. I haven't yet found a jeweler who could repair it but I haven't given up. For now, I just enjoy wearing it as a pendant on a chain. I always get compliments on it.

Whenever I look at this quaint little antique timepiece, I remember the beautiful free-spirited woman who wore it those many years ago. She taught me many things but the most important lesson I learned was by her example….to love life and to enjoy it to the fullest. Thank you, Mamaw!

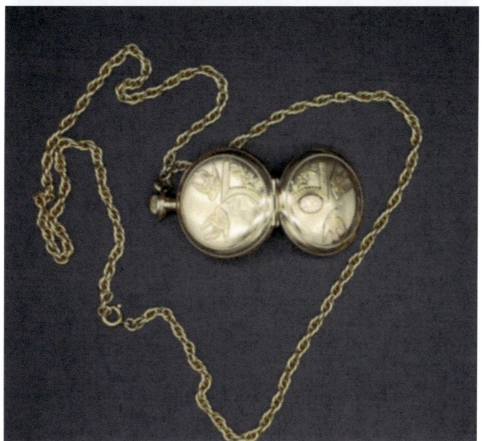

1931 Was A Very Good Year
Mac Booth

My keepsake is my 1931 Chevrolet Cabriolet. Although I've only had her for five years, our relationship goes back to my birth. First let me tell you about her. The 1931 Chevy model was distinctive. It offered the new 6-cylinder engine as standard equipment. The "fast" 50-horsepower engine was advertised to give 25 per cent more power than the engine in any other car of equally low price. (Can you say Ford?) And it could go from 0 to 35 mph in 6.7 seconds. Additionally, the car is a beauty with rakish lines, sparkling colors, and handsome Fisher body coachwork. Chevrolet advertised that the prices ran as low as $475.

I bought her in 2014 from a guy in Maine. I always wanted an old car, one as old as me. Well I got what I wished for. She was built in 1931, the year of my birth. She was built in Atlanta, Georgia; I was born in Atlanta, Georgia. The engine was built in one part of Atlanta and the body was built by Fisher Body in another part of Atlanta. My father worked for Fisher Body, so he had a hand in the building of my car. How neat is that? Maybe it was destiny, I don't know, but you can see we were meant for each other.

Right now, she is in the hospital. Her parts, like many of ours, are old and need repairs. That "fast" 50-horsepower engine has lost much of its get up and go and is being rebuilt so it can generate enough power to climb the hills around Longhorn Village. But she's still a beauty and gets lots of looks when she's out on the road. Let me know if you want to go for a ride.

Souvenirs from China
Orville Brauss

I was a Second Lieutenant during World War II. After the atomic bomb was dropped and the war was officially declared over, my company was sent to China to pick up prisoners of war. The Chinese were happy to see us and showed us their gratitude by giving us gifts. One little girl gave me a small Chinese flag. An elderly man gave me a beautiful black silk robe that was over 100 years old. I was also given a silver cigarette box and cigarette holder. They are my keepsakes.

Christmas Angels
Bob Carnes

In 1962, we were preparing to celebrate our first Christmas together. Roberta was a student in college and I was a young Lieutenant in the Marine Corps. Times were lean and money was scarce. We purchased a set of angels for twenty-nine cents at the checkout stand of a drug store as our first and what would be our only Christmas decoration that year.

Since then, we have moved 19 times and celebrated Christmas throughout the world. The little angels have always been a prominent part of our annual decorations.

Mother's Love
Roberta Irene Carnes

My mother was a very private person. She was unable to express or receive affection easily. She recoiled from touch, except from my father. There was never an open demonstration of affection between her and myself or my brothers.

One day, when I was a teenager, we took friends sightseeing in San Juan Capistrano and as we were passing a curio window, my mother apparently observed me admiring a small Hummel figurine. It was of a hooded little girl holding an orange pot of flowers. Imagine my surprise when I received that little figurine on the next gift-giving occasion. I had not openly expressed a desire for the figurine, but when I received it, I knew she loved me. It sits on my nightstand to this day as a reminder of her love.

Portrait of Abraham Lincoln
Bill Chambless

My keepsake is a portrait of Abraham Lincoln that was done by Matthew Wilson two weeks before the assassination. In those days, artists were commissioned to paint a portrait, but the artist often made copies (original paintings that were copies of the original), and Wilson made several copies that were hung in the Navy Department, or given to friends of the sponsor, Gideon Welles, Lincoln's Secretary of the Navy.

It is said that the painting shows a "hint of merriment" in Lincoln's face, "perhaps a reflection of the fact that Grant was scoring victories and the war might soon be over.

My wife bought the painting at an estate sale in Amarillo, Texas in the '60's. We are not sure of its originality or history. We just liked it and hauled it from place to place in our many moves. We have always enjoyed looking at it and proudly displayed it.

Dad and Uncle Eric
Sonia Colorito

My keepsake is a photo of my father and uncle taken on July 3, 1907. The photo is in a maple desktop frame of that era. My father, Elmer Olander, was born in the United States. My uncle, Eric, was born in Sweden. Their mother (my Grandmother) died when my father was 6. Their father worked for the railroad and was away from home most of the time. After their mother's death, their Aunt Louise took them to live with her where she worked at Chaddock Boy's School, a military school, in Quincy, Illinois. During the summers, the boys lived with relatives in Iowa.

My father worked for Scott Foresman and Company, an educational publishing company best known for the "**Dick and Jane**" stories. My father was an editor and later supervised the printing division.

The picture frame has been on my dresser for many years; the photo, protected by a childhood picture of me and my brother, when we were 3 and 5. But my father and uncle are right behind, so I will never forget them. Knowing their picture is in the frame reminds me of the cohesiveness of their extended family.

A Parents' Life-line
Gareth and Janie Cook

It isn't beautiful or artistic or even unique in any way, but it is treasured for the time in our lives that it represents. Our keepsake is a simple, small microcassette recorder.

In 1996, when our daughter, Laurie, graduated from college, she went to Niger, West Africa as a Peace Corps volunteer. She and about 20 other young women went together to the capital, Niamey, where they spent 3 months training to be maternal and child health volunteers. After training they were each assigned to a village where they lived and worked for the next two years. Only 1/3 of that group finished their full two-year service.

Laurie was assigned to Dan Tchaio, a village that was an all-day bus ride from the capital and about 4 kilometers from the Nigerian border. She worked in and around her village to encourage family planning, healthy pregnancy, safe delivery and infant nutrition. Her means of travel was a motorcycle that she had to learn to repair and to push for a mile in deep sand in order to get her license. She communicated in the local language, Hausa, and lived without a phone, running water or electricity. At that time, Niger had the highest mortality rate for women and children in the world.

For us to talk to her, she had to go to a village several hours away where there was a phone. These calls happened by pre-arranged appointment because she couldn't afford to call us, so we had to call her. This is the way it worked. At an undetermined time about every 6-8 weeks, we would receive a call from another Peace Corps parent in the US who relayed a message to us that we were to call her on a specific day at a specific time. Needless to say, those were highly anticipated phone calls that only lasted a few precious minutes. The first thing we always heard from her was, "Hi Mom and Dad, I'm happy and healthy and here is the Peace Corps family you need to call when we hang up." So, we were part of a Peace Corps Parent life-line that snaked across the US. Given the difficulty of talking with her directly by phone, we relied on letters and shared microcassettes by mail. She would record herself telling us about what she was experiencing, put that in the mail and we would get it 2-3 weeks later. As a parent knows, hearing your child's voice tells you volumes that words cannot communicate. So, these little cassettes were a vital link that connected our hearts. Each time we listened to one, we could take a deep breath as we heard her voice and were reassured she was okay.

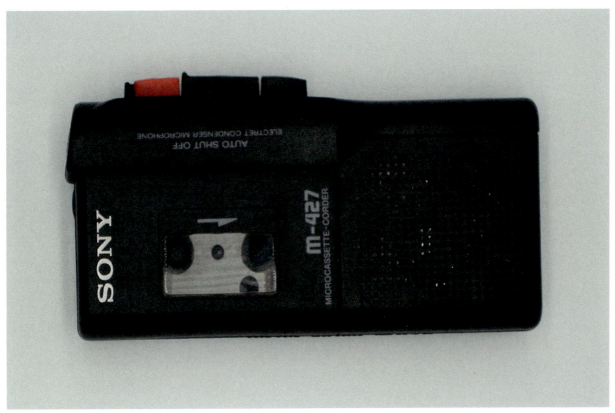

Pickett Slide Rule
Dick Corlett

My keepsake is a 1962 Pickett slide rule and 1953 manual. After service in the Marine Corps, I started studying for a Bachelor's degree in Construction Engineering at Arizona State University. It was an absolute necessity for courses such as Strength in Materials, Estimating, Physics, and other engineering classes. I also used it in Finance classes. I've kept it because it taught me to use simple logic in checking my answers by determining if they were reasonable. Also, because it was used in other important engineering projects. For example, it was used in early space exploration and helped us get to the moon and back. I wouldn't part with it and I'm guessing that other engineers at Longhorn Village have theirs in a drawer somewhere.

My Father's Painting
Pat Corlett

The special keepsake that I have is a painting that my father, John L. Greene, did in 1953, when I was 10 years old. It is an abstract expressionist painting in the style of Jackson Pollock. I remember watching him doing it on the floor of our living room and observing his thoughtfulness when choosing the colors. He fussed over each pour and explained that he would "just know" when it was finished. If he didn't like something, he would get a window squeegee, wipe it off, and start over. I was fascinated by the whole process. I admired him for his creativity in art, his sense of humor, and his writing. Just thinking of him makes me happy. Having it in my home gives me pleasure daily and I want to pass it on to my children.

Time in a Bottle
Norris Couch

My wife and I visited Beijing, China in April of 2007 as part of a post-cruise land package. On the 3rd day in Beijing, we visited the Great Wall. Our initial starting point was very crowded so I decided to walk to a guard tower away from the crowd. Upon arriving at this location, I discovered a vendor/woman, who was selling uniquely painted bottles. Every day she had to carry her materials to this location, set up her equipment, and perform her craft. I was impressed by her grit and wanted to buy one of her bottles. She painted beautiful scenes inside these small bottles error free. She customized the scene in the bottles if you bought one. It took a while to communicate what I wanted to be written but once she understood, she did it quickly and easily with a small brush with bristles that were bent at a 90-degree angle and ending in a point. Here is what the little bottle looks like. I was pleased she added our names and the date, 4/11/07. I keep this bottle as a memento of our trip and memory of my wife, Diane.

Horse Reins
Judy Creveling

When I was a child, at every Christmas, Easter, birthday, and other gift-giving occasions, and even at bed-time prayers, I asked for a horse. And it finally happened. When I was nine years old, my father, Fred Hoepfner, bought me a big, beautiful white horse that I named "Prince." We had a farm and a ranch and I rode Prince whenever I could.

In addition to buying a saddle, bridle, and other tack, my father had bridle reins made of woven horsehair. They were the most beautiful reins I had ever seen; I saw them as a work of art. Today, they are worn, and frayed, but I still prize them; they are a precious keepsake. They remind me of a wonderful time in my life. They represent for me my happy childhood and the trust and encouragement given by a loving parent.

Frascati Pearls
Mary Jo Culver

My husband, John Culver, and I had a great trip to Italy in 2004. After spending a few days in Rome, we decided to visit the town of Frascati, south of Rome. Frascati is famous for its notable villas and wine. We took a train and bus to get there, and during our wandering I discovered a shop with lovely pearls. I picked out the strand and the clasp and was told they would be ready in a couple of hours.

But our credit card would not go through and we could not purchase the pearls without a passport. But of course, we did not take it for a day trip! As only John would have said: "Okay, let's go back to Rome and get it." So off to the bus and train back to the hotel. Got the passport and took the train and bus back to Frascati. I treasure them and treasure that wonderful, kind, thoughtful man.

Skydiving Practice

47

1958 Packard Hawk
Morris Davies

My keepsake is a 1958 Packard Hawk. I always wanted an old car; something unique, something unlike those that others had The Packard Hawk is my dream come true. I bought her in 1967 or 68. A guy advertised that he was going in the army and needed to sell his car. She was my dream come true. It was love at first sight, and I bought her. The car needed a lot of work, so I stored her until 2000 and then I had her restored. It's a very unique car for lots of reasons. Let me begin by describing her.

First of all, she's a glorious machine. In 1956, Packard and Studebaker merged and the 1958 Packard Hawk was basically a Studebaker Golden Hawk 400 with a fiberglass front end and a modified deck lid. Instead of a grill, it has a wide, low opening above the bumper that covers the entire width of the front of the car.

The 1958 Packard version was a one-year wonder. It was the final year of the Packard brand, a once prestigious American automobile manufacturer founded in 1899. Because Packard disappeared after 1958, the 1958 Packard Hawk was a one-year only production car. That almost automatically made it collectible from the get-go. To add to that, only 588 Packard Hawks were ever made. Bingo. Instant collector status. Mine is one of the only four made that were painted with a "Mountain Blue" body, a "Waterfall Blue" top, gold anodized mylar inlays on the outsize surface of the fins, and exterior leather armrests.

New Packard Hawk buyers paid $3,995 for the privilege of ownership. Options, including power steering, brakes, windows and seat and more exciting stuff, could push the final price to near $5,000. A six-tube, manually-tuned AM radio was available for $60.50 and those who could afford to go another $19.40 could get a SEVEN-TUBE radio with push-button tuning. A pair of "safety belts" (front seat only) was offered for an additional $24.95. Today, Packard Hawks sell for over $100,000.

Finally, my 1958 Packard Hawk has been recognized by others as a beauty. In 2008, she won Best of Show at the Rock Hall Vintage Car Show and first place in the national Studebaker car show in Lancaster, Pennsylvania. So, you can see why my keepsake is special to me.

Linen Envelope
Anita Davis

I was born in Latvia during World War II. I was four, when my family fled Latvia and we were forced to live in camps for displaced persons. For health reasons, when I was eight, I was sent to a girls' boarding school in Brussels. My parents remained in a DP camp in Germany.

Although being separated from my parents was sad, the girls' school was wonderful. I learned, not only academics, but also fine arts for young ladies, including embroidery. While there I embroidered a white linen envelope with the initial of my first name "A," proudly displayed in the middle, a windmill in the left corner, and a girl with a broom in the other corner. Among other things, I stored my ribbons that anchored my braids in it. Also tucked in was a treasured letter from my parents.

When we sailed from Bremerhaven to Ellis Island, it housed the keepsakes that I brought with me to America. As displaced persons, our priorities were mostly about staying alive and did not include gifts and presents. Imagine how I felt when I received a scarf as a present in my first Christmas in Iowa. I don't remember ever wearing it and I thought it rather ugly, but it was my first Christmas present and I kept it in my little linen treasure, frequently running my fingers over it to feel its silky, smooth texture.

Over the years, this little linen envelope has contained many things including a few love letters from my first serious crush, who I met at a debate at the University of Iowa. Safely hidden from a nosy sister, this well-worn piece of linen, allowed me to read and re-read them to my heart's content. It also held a hand-made hanker-chief that my grandmother gave me; she never liked Kleenex. When I married, it was the keeper of the exquisite strand of pearls my husband gave me on our wedding day.

I've kept this old linen envelope through all my moves and down-sizing. I don't use it to hold material things anymore. Now it only holds memories. But then, that's what I treasure most of all.

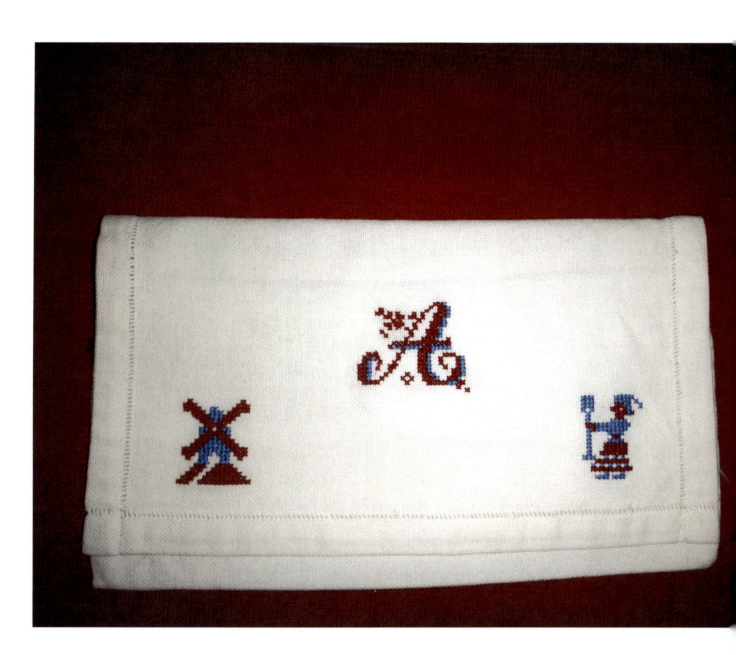

Aunt Dorothy's Handkerchiefs
Pat Davis

Times were tough during the years of the Great Depression and everyone was affected one way or another. My parents took in Mom's Father, Mother, and Sister. They lived with us for many years, occupying the basement of our home in Denver, Colorado. Mom and her sister, my Aunt Dorothy, were very close and they enjoyed being with each other and making each other laugh. They used to give each other funny poems that they wrote. Here's an example;

> *Here's a ditty, short and sweet,*
> *With a handkerchief folded neat,*
> *Witty words just will not come*
> *S'pose its 'cause I am so dumb.*
> *I've thought and thought and sighed and sighed!*
> *Anyway, you can see I tried.*
> *Hope you had a Happy Day.*
> *Hope all in '61 will be that way.*
> *Love,*
> *Sis*

Every year, at Christmas time, they would exchange poems and fancy handkerchiefs. After Granddaddy finished his breakfast, we would gather around the Christmas tree and we would exchange presents. We all looked forward to hearing Mom and Aunt Dorothy read their poems to each other. I have a collection of their poems and some of their handkerchiefs, they are my special keepsakes

To Misha, With Love, Dad
Mische Dey

My father was in the army during World War II and was stationed in London. He sent this necklace to me when I was 2 years old, and I have kept it ever since as a reminder of him. Before the war, he worked in a prison in Indiana and might have been involved in that work during the war. After the war was over, he went on to get a Ph.D. in clinical psychology from Duke University. He taught at Duke and the University of Florida until he retired.

The spelling on the pendant is interesting; "Misha." My name is actually Myra Marische and I was nicknamed "Misha." But I've always spelled my name, "Mische." I really don't know why there are different spellings.

I wore the necklace in high school but didn't wear it much as an adult. I plan to give it to my daughter, when I pass on.

He Was My Friend
Dub Dickson

El Onizuka was a friend of mine. You probably know him better as one of the astronauts who died when the Space Shuttle **Challenger** exploded 73 seconds after launch. My keepsake is one of the flight-suit uniform patches that he took with him on that tragic flight. Before I tell you about my keepsake, I want to tell you about El, and how I knew him.

Ellison Shoji Onizuka was born in 1946 in Hawaii and earned his B.S. and M.S. at the University of Colorado in 1969, where he was in the U.S. Air Force ROTC program. After joining the Air Force in 1970, he served as a test pilot and flight test engineer. He was selected for the astronaut program in 1978, worked on test teams, launch support crews, and flew on the Space Shuttle **Discovery** in 1985. He had a total of 74 hours in space.

El and I became friends when he was stationed in Houston. At the time, I was Director of the International committee of the Houston Livestock Show and Rodeo. El came to visit and I showed him around and we became good friends. On his first shuttle trip, he carried my wedding ring with him and returned it to me as a souvenir of his space voyage. Our families were close and we often visited each other. Before the Challenger flight, he insisted that I bring the family to Cape Canaveral to let him show us around. We spent a week there, but it was miserably cold and there wasn't a lot to do so we decided to fly back home. When we got back, we received the news that the shuttle had blown up and El was killed along with the other astronauts.

Before the shuttle launch, I gave El some badges from the livestock show that he was to bring back for me. He also took a bunch of flight-suit uniform patches and other items. Everything was registered and certified as being on the flight. Following the disaster, the shuttle's cockpit and El's "Personal Egress Air Packs" and those of the pilot, Michael Smith and mission specialist, Judith Resnik were recovered. After the funeral, the patches I had given him were returned to me, along with some of the flight-suit uniform patches; mine being one of them. I will always treasure the patch as a remembrance of my remarkable friend.

Shirley Temple Doll
Sondra Durso

My aunt and uncle gave me this Shirley Temple doll in 1937 or 1938 for my birthday. She was a huge Hollywood star during my childhood. I watched all of her movies and wanted to take dancing lessons to be like her. The clothes she is wearing in the photo are original clothes that came with the doll. It was always on display in our house, but because it was so special, I was not allowed to play with it. My parents were worried that I might break it.

The chair the doll is standing on was my mother's. It came from her church. She used to sit on it during Sunday School. When the church was closed, my grandparents bought it from the church and gave it to my mother. My sister and I used it often, especially for tea parties. It has had little use since then. My boys didn't use it but my grand-daughter used it with her dolls.

It Just Caught My Eye
Frank Ely

My keepsake is a mantle clock I got in 1958 at an auction in Hampton, Virginia. I saw the clock in the pre-auction viewing and something about it caught my eye. It was dirty and didn't run but for some reason, it attracted me. I talked with the auctioneer and he said it probably wouldn't be sold because there was no interest in it. He said there needed to be at least two bidders or he couldn't sell it. So, I looked around and found a guy and told him that I wanted him to bid on it (but not too much) and not to worry because he wouldn't win. And he didn't. I won the auction bidding $35.00.

I had a neighbor who liked to work on clocks and he cleaned it up and got it running and it has run well for sixty years.

The clock is heavy, weighing about 40 pounds. It has gold markings on the front and inlays of lapis lazuli. Also prominent are two rubies on the pendulum. It chimes on the hour and half-hour. It is a well-constructed time piece.

As an Air Force Officer, we moved often and always carried the clock with us, not trusting it to movers. About 10 years ago, I took it to a clock maker who advised me to insure it for at least $10,000. And just think, I was the only one interested in it at the auction.

Bling, Bling, Bling
Joan Ely

When I was a young girl, my mother managed an upscale condo-townhome facility in San Antonio. Two sisters from St. Paul, Minnesota lived there and they became close friends with my Mom and Dad. I met them twice when I visited there. Their residence was like a boutique with so many beautiful and expensive things. They were obviously very wealthy. They were always exquisitely dressed to the nines.

One of the sisters, Reene, was hospitalized for something and died in the hospital. After her estate was settled, my mother received a call informing her that she and I inherited some jewelry. My mother called to inform me that she had some important news for me. The bad news was that Reene had passed away; the good news was she left me this beautiful diamond ring.

I have no clue why she left me such an extraordinary ring. My mother and I were the only people to receive such gifts. The ring is truly awesome. It is the most valuable piece of jewelry I own. It has a 3-carat marquise diamond encircled by 40 diamonds in a sunburst pattern. To me, it is a perfect example of Bling and I love it. I wear it nearly every evening. It reminds me of both Reene and my mother. I am going to pass it on to my daughter.

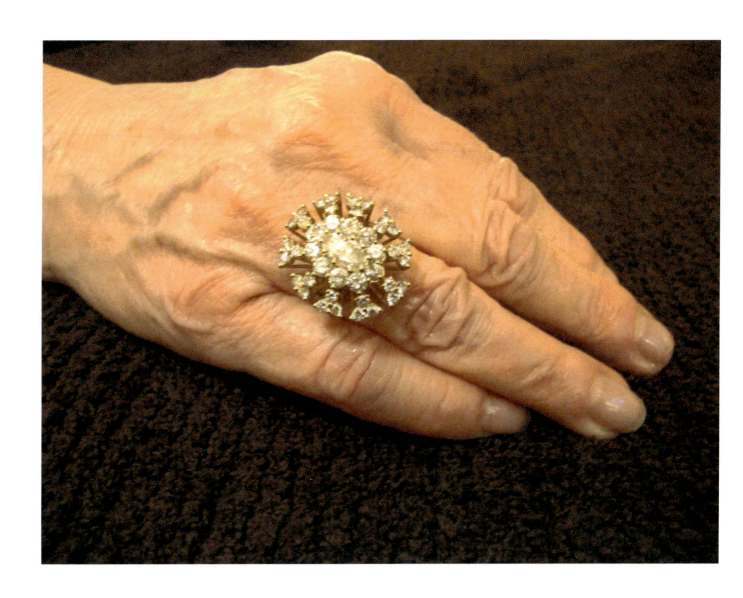

Getting Stoned
Lois Evans

Stones are my keepsakes. I am fascinated by their shape, color, lines. In some way, they remind me of my grandfather who was a stone mason. He did beautiful work with stones and it was truly an art form. As a young man, he was taught by the masons of Europe and worked with them on cathedrals, major city buildings, and repairing the Appian Way.

Stones are intriguing to me. Wherever I go, I always keep my eye out for them. I have boxes of them. I feel like I am connected to my grandfather because of the stones.

Lowrey Organ
Paul Evans

My keepsake is my Lowrey organ. I have had it about five years and it is magnificent. It is not only a great musical instrument but it is beautiful as well. It is a virtual orchestra. It plays like a piano but is all digital, and provides harmonics, rhythms, and interesting background effects. It's like a computer in the sense that there are so many things it can do if you learn how to do them. There is so much to learn. Although I am an amateur player without formal training, I like playing music. I started out playing the trombone as a kid, and I've been playing the organ for quite a few years. Playing music that I'm familiar with is relaxing and it is challenging when I work on new things. It gives me a sense of satisfaction. I feel happy when I play, especially when Lois is listening, and she is happy when she hears me play.

Engagement Dog
Jan Everett

Don Dilday came to Baylor University our Sophomore year, transferring after an injury that ended a promising football career. We met in Sociology class, then went out for coffee, dated and became lifelong friends. As seniors, we were featured in the annual as "Who's Whose at Baylor," and he later proposed. Lacking funds for a proper ring, Don carved this little cartoon-like dog, and presented it while kneeling on one knee. We married later that year, and had a wonderful, 40-year run until his death in 1993. It was a toy for our two boys, and was replaced with a lovely ring some years later, but is still a much-loved treasure that stays nearby through a lifetime of good memories.

Buffalo Bill Cody's Horse's Bridle Bit
Jerry Fineg

My father was a collector of Western memorabilia and somehow acquired this bit from the bridle of Buffalo Bill Cody's horse. I got the bit from him just before he died. It is the only piece I have from his collection, so it is special to me.

The bit is interesting, not only because it belonged to Buffalo Bill, but because of how it was made. Manufactured by North and Judd, a famous maker of saddlery hardware, the bit is made of brass, nickel, and steel and is very heavy. It weighs two pounds. It is engraved with the name, "W.F. Cody" on the brass just below the cylinder. His horse had to be big and strong to hold such a large bit. I'm not sure of the name of the horse but I think it might have been Isham, the horse he used in the last of his Wild West Shows. I wish I had seen Buffalo Bill in one of his shows but he died in 1917, before I was born. Still, I have something to remind me of him and my father; two special men.

Wife, Whiff, Woof,
Bob Freeman

There have been three major forces in my life; music, baseball, and dogs. My wonderful wife Carol was integral to all three. I have a baseball, given to me by her that has great meaning to me. I was not much of a baseball player as a kid. I think my greatest accomplishment in the fourth grade was to hit into a ground out. Nevertheless, I have always loved the game. From 1975 to 1977, I was the coach of the Little League team that my son played on in Rochester, New York and I'm proud to say that we were undefeated during two of the seasons. Carol attended the games and after one game in 1975 presented me with this ball. On it she wrote, *"Coach Freeman, I love you - May I be on your team always - Carol."* I wrote on the other side of the ball, *"Dear Sweet Wife, You will always be my only team mate. I love you. Bob."* The ball always occupied a prominent place wherever we lived. It is my most precious keepsake.

Carol and I were married for forty-two wonderful years. She passed away in 2018. I wrote a book, ***Woof! A Love Story of Dogs, Music, and Life*** and dedicated it to her. The book, the ball, and our dogs bonded us together. And all remind me of her.

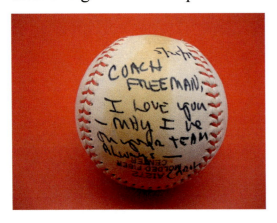
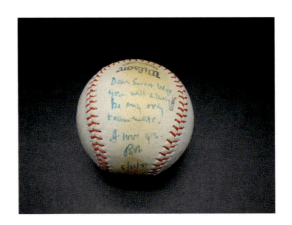

My First Pair of Shoes
Jim Gilliam

I have no memory of my early years from birth to age five. Many years ago, I wrote my Mother and asked her to write about what significant events occurred during those early years and what things were formative in determining who I am today. My Mother responded with a lengthy narrative about things that were happening from my birth to age 5, but most of the things she wrote about were things that were happening to her during this time period. She included these baby shoes in the envelope which contained her story.

    I'm not sure why I still have them. I think they speak to me about my life and things that I no longer remember. They offer suggestions as to what life might have been like long before I knew anything about anything. Like I noted previously, I have no memories of myself at the age when I would have

worn these shoes. The condition of the leather, the holes in the toes, the worn, scuffed sides and soles suggest that they were worn for a long time and that maybe I still wore them even after they were too small for me.

    Many people had their baby shoes bronzed and mounted as a keepsake. My mother probably didn't have the money to have them mounted, but I'm glad she saved them for me. They are now my keepsake.

My Baby Bracelet
Judith Gilliam

I have always known that this small, gold, baby bracelet engraved with "Judy" was given to me by my great-grandfather Luther Garrett. My grandmother was his first child and my father was his first grandchild and I was his first great-grandchild. That was all I knew. I didn't learn the rest of the story until recently when I did my family tree on Ancestry.com. I was contacted by a person who thought that we might be related and had an old photo of four people in a small boat. He knew the name of the older man, who was Luther Garrett, and asked for my help in identifying the other three people. I immediately recognized my grandparents and the location where the photo was taken and began to put the story together.

The older woman in the boat was my grandmother's stepmother. My grandmother's mother died when she was two years old in 1898. My great-grandfather lived in Sullivan, Illinois and had journeyed to Michigan, where his daughter lived, to see me and attend my baptism in October 1941. This is when he gave me the bracelet. On this trip my grandparents took the couple to see the lake property that my grandfather owned and maybe enjoy the beautiful fall color. He returned soon after to Illinois and died two years later at 78 years old. I am happy to have the photo of him on my grandfather's boat having fun just like I did when I was a child.

My keepsake, the bracelet, represents a link between the small child I once was, the woman I am today, and my family who loved me.

Treasure of Love
Mary Juan Harris

One of my most treasured possessions is a hand-stitched quilt that my maternal grandmother made for my mother when she was a baby. My grandmother, Mary Briley Morgan, was born in 1878 in Northern California. She moved several times in a covered wagon from California to Oklahoma and then to Crowley, Texas. She and my grandfather, J.T. Morgan, had four children. My mother, born in 1909, was the youngest.

Growing up, my special treat was visiting with grandma and grandpa Morgan for a week. Their life was so different from how I lived in the big city of Dallas. They had an out-house, storm cellar, and chicken coop. Lacking in most "luxuries," they were happy in their rural life and grandma loved to quilt. I am proud that I got my name from my grandmother, Mary, and my mother, Juanita.

After I married and moved to Lufkin, Texas, I followed in my mother's footsteps of teaching and counseling. On my 45th birthday, I received a huge surprise. My mother presented me with her baby quilt that grandmother Morgan had made for her. All these years, mother had the quilt but I had never seen it. For my birthday, she had the quilt framed and gave it to me. We hung it in our living room over our piano. It has always been my special treasure of LOVE. When I moved to Longhorn Village, my son found the perfect spot for it; over my bed. I feel blessed with this special treasure of LOVE.

Shadow Box of Legacies
Teresa Harris

The mementos in this shadow box are just a small reminder of the rich and full lives that my parents led. From my mom's being a go-getter in the realm of her career, her educational pursuits for herself and for the community in which she lived, her political aspirations, her devotion to her family, an excellent cook and most of all, to her faith in Christ. She lived a full life!

My father was devoted to his family. It was just my brother and me, and he made sure that we wanted for nothing. He was a welder by trade, a small business owner, a constant stream of encouragement but most important to him was his faith in Christ which he showed to us in various ways every day. Dad was a disciplinarian but he ruled with fairness and love. I felt that love always; no matter what was going on in our lives. He lived a full life!

When I look at this shadow box, I see two people who stood steadfast through the good and bad times and a wealth of memories and emotions flood me to my core. The sad smile it brings to my face pales in comparison to remembering the legacy they left their children and grandchildren. A legacy of faith in Christ, strength, determination, perseverance, and unconditional love. We weren't rich with money but we were rich with what counted in life and for that I say: "Thanks mom and dad! Job well done!"

Guam was the Pitts
Al Heilbrun

My keepsake is a memory I have that goes back to World War II. In 1945, I had just graduated from Officer Candidate School in the United States Marine Corps. I joined my battalion in San Diego and we sailed west headed for Guam. We were to use Guam for staging for the invasion of Japan. While we were at sea the atomic bomb was dropped on Hiroshima and Nagasaki and before we reached Guam, the war was over.

As a new, young Second Lieutenant, I was given the most menial duties beyond my role as platoon leader. I was put in charge of beer distribution for our unit. Guam was oppressively hot, but my men did not want to drink the beer we had for them. The beer, Fort Pitt, was warm, green in color, and tasted terrible. The men hated it. The cans kept piling up and after two months took on the appearance of the tallest mountain on Guam. When we shipped out for Japan, our next destination, we left a huge mountain of unopened Fort Pitt beer cans. I often wonder if that mound is still there.

In closing, I want you to know that I was discharged from the Corps in 1946 but was recalled for the Korean War where I was used in a more military fashion as a platoon leader near the 38th parallel. You might be interested to know that another Longhorn Village resident, Orville Brauss, was my company commander in Korea.

Well, that's my story. That's my Keepsake.

My Baby Grand
Marian Heilbrun

My keepsake is my 1929 Steinway Model L Baby Grand piano. A rich lady in Iowa City, Iowa ordered it with special bowed legs. I don't think she played it; she just bought it for its looks. A neighbor of hers was a friend of ours and she told us the lady was selling her house with the piano. The lady thought we would be perfect for the house and the piano would be perfect for me. She asked us to make her an offer, we did, she took it, and we became the proud owners of a new house and baby grand piano. The piano has been a wonderful addition to our family for all these years. I play it every day and it gives me a warm, joyful feeling. My daughter will inherit when I'm gone.

Flapper, Yes Sir, One of Those!
Peg Hein

When I was in college, I went to a dance with my parents, and to my surprise, I saw my mother doing the Charleston. I asked her if she was a "Flapper," and she said, "I suppose so. I've drunk my share of bathtub gin." She lived in Amarillo during the twenties and thirties but she never talked about that era.

After Mom died, I read her diary and I discovered that she had an active social life. It seemed from what I read that she enjoyed dating, dancing, and partying. Her diary indicated she attended many balls, country club dances, and soirees. She must have been gorgeous in her flapper era clothes, some of which are my keepsakes which you can see in the accompanying photographs.

My father met and married mom after her flapper days. He was my hero. He was tall, good looking, with wavy, white hair. He was elegant, classy, and always immaculately dressed. His silver cigarette case and letter opener make me think of him as a kind of F. Scott Fitzgerald. He was my saving grace; my hero. He became my step-father when I was 10 years old. He managed a resort hotel in Minnesota and later was a real estate salesman. My keepsakes bring back memories of both of them.

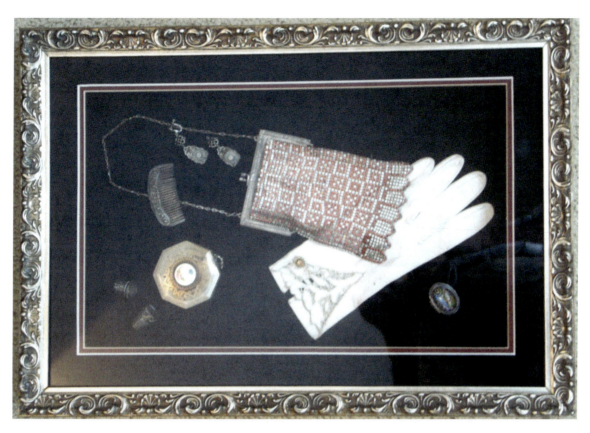

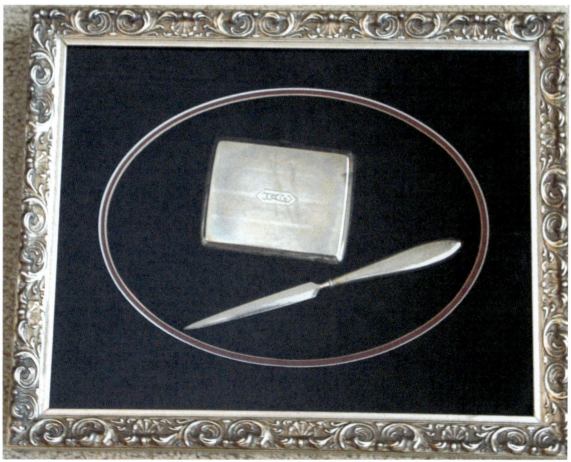

Our Rings
John and Charlotte Henderson

Both of our keepsakes are the rings that we wear all the time. They are very special to us. Charlotte and John were married in 1939. John will tell his story first.

I played football for The University of Texas from 1932 until 1935 and I am proud to say that I am the oldest living football player from UT. Many, many years after my football career was over, Coach Darrell K. Royal began the tradition of awarding a T-Ring to each football player who lettered for two years and graduated. When I read about this practice in the *Alcalde*, I called an athletic council member and said, "Can old-timers get a ring too?" He said, "You can buy one." So, I bought mine and I've worn it ever since. The rules today are somewhat different. Any UT athlete (not just football players) who earns two letters in a sport and graduates is awarded a T-Ring.

Charlotte: My diamond ring was given to me by my mother. She received it from my father as a birthday gift or wedding anniversary present; I don't remember which. She had two diamond rings and gave one to me and one to my sister. I don't remember when she gave it to me. Mine is my favorite ring and I wear it all the time. Although, it was given to me by my parents as a wedding gift, I think of it as coming from John.

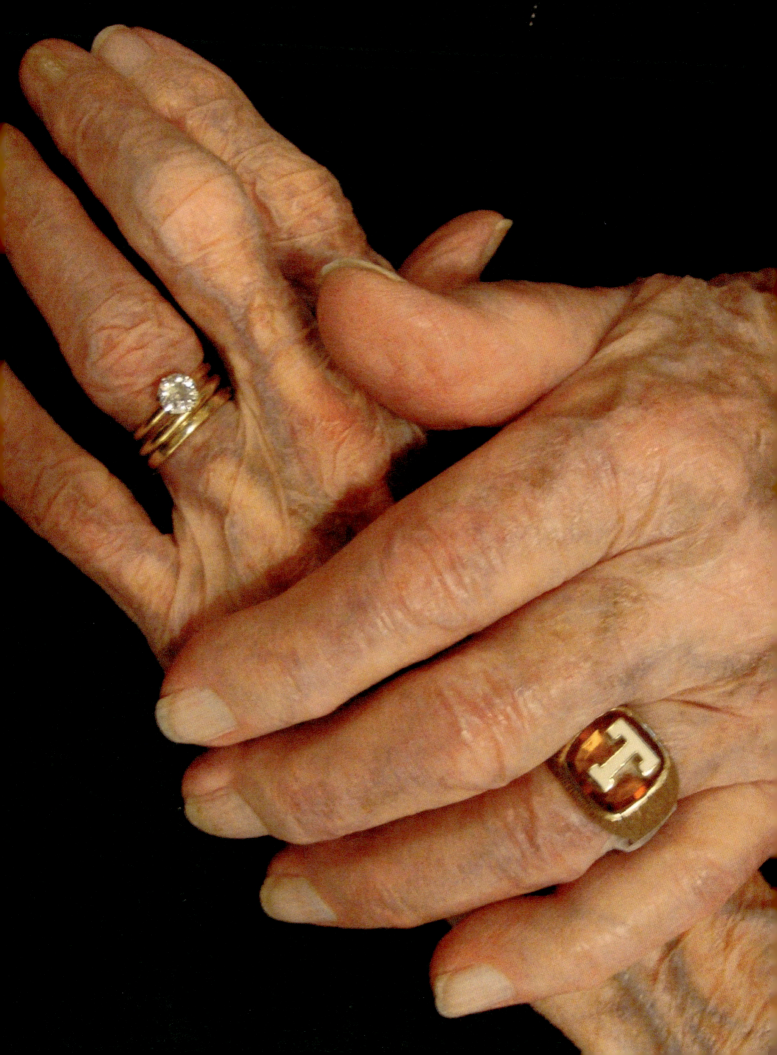

All Tied-Up
Jim Henegar

I was a business manager for ARCO petroleum company for 35 years and at my retirement, I was given this hand-stitched quilt. It was made by my secretary. Unbeknownst to me, she had been acquiring ties from the different men who worked with me. She meticulously took them apart, washed them, ironed them, and then pieced them into this quilt. Some of the ties were mine but I had no idea my wife had been secreting them to her. I have no idea of how many ties are in the quilt.

I have a strong, sentimental attachment to this quilt. My secretary was a very special, caring person who worked diligently for me and the company. I am reminded of her every time I look at it. I don't know who I will pass it on to.

The Indomitable Lady
Pat Hime

I treasure the book "*Indomitable Lady*" which is a biography of Blanche Groves who was my Dad's cousin. Blanche was born in 1889, grew up in Bridgeport, Texas and after graduating from Decatur Baptist College and Baylor University volunteered to go to Soochow, China in 1920 as a missionary. She remained there until 1942 when she (along with other missionaries) was escorted by Japanese officials to Shanghai and put on a boat back to the U. S. In February 1946, she returned to Soochow to work in the missionary field again until 1952. After two years in Honolulu, she returned to Hong Kong where she lived and worked until 1958. She moved back to her hometown of Bridgeport at age 69.

She was a woman of great strength and belief in God and through pain and fear she endured to teach and minister to the people of China. Her faith was unbounded.

I am proud to be related to Blanche Groves and this book about her is my treasured keepsake.

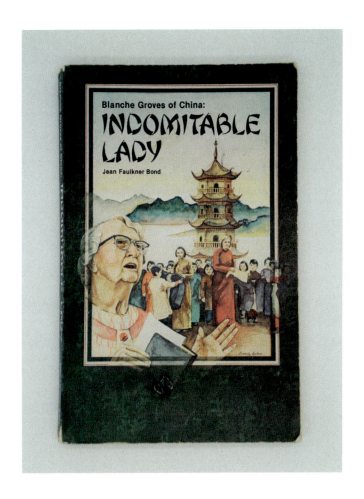

My Father's Watch
Curt Holleman

My father retired as CFO from an often-struggling Michigan company in 1978. He was given a nice but not extremely expensive watch at his retirement party. As one who appreciated goods that performed and never caused problems, he became very fond of that watch. Both he and I thought that it was a very good looking as well as dependable watch.

When my father died in 2005, the watch that I had been wearing quit on me that same week. I am one of four brothers, and none of us wanted more than a couple of keepsakes from my parents. Since my watch had just stopped running, I asked for my father's watch. My mother thought it was especially fitting that I inherit it, because of the four brothers I was the one who most resembled my father in appearance and temperament. So, it became mine.

As time has passed, I have mistakenly worn the watch swimming, I have worn it playing vigorous sports, and young acquaintances have subjected it to special abuse. Despite the abuse, it has distinguished itself by never needing a battery and never getting as much as one minute off true time as long as I have had it. The watch itself is an "Eco-Drive" and powered by any kind of light, not just solar.

After an encounter with a young neighbor who broke the watchband while playing with it, I took my treasured watch to a jeweler. Before replacing the watchband, I asked how long the watch should last and how costly it would be to fix it if the watch itself broke. The jeweler said the mechanism in watches like this should last about twenty years, and they are very difficult to fix and replace.

I am happy to say that this watch is now forty-one years old, having lasted more than twice its projected lifetime. Although I have more treasured memories of life with my father, this is my most treasured physical memory, and it is an extra joy that it has so greatly outperformed its projected life.

My Father's Ship
Ruth Holleman

Many years ago, my parents, due to their frail health, needed to move into a nursing home. They were limited in what they could take to their new space and my siblings and I had to decide what we would like to keep before the rest of their furnishings were sold in an estate sale. Since I lived the furthest away (my parents lived in Michigan), I had to choose items that I could easily transport or send back to my home in Dallas, Texas. Without hesitation, my first choice was a model of a ship. The ship had been given to Dad when he was a young man by one of his friends who traveled the world. That ship was always displayed prominently in our home and I knew it meant a great deal to him.

I wish I knew more about the provenance of this ship; however, the fact that it was loved so much by my dad meant and means everything to me. Since the ship came to live with me, it has been on display in Dallas, Blanco, Cedar Park, and now Longhorn Village in Austin. It is extremely old and very fragile. We no longer can attempt to dust it since the sails crack so easily. This ship reminds me on a daily basis of my love for my dad and mom and their love for me and my brother and sister.

Noah's Ark
Judith Infante

My keepsake is a small sculpture (6"x 6") representing Noah's Ark. Made of hand-potted clay, it is in the tradition of the Tree-of-Life sculptures popular in Mexican folk art. By twos, tiny, colorful animals, birds, and butterflies inhabit a dense backdrop of greenery and flowers. A sweet-faced sun rises, and above it, the arc of rainbow, and above the rainbow, the stars!

In 1970, I moved with my husband and daughters to Mexico City. Right away I realized that we would be living in a country with one of the most exciting cultural and artistic traditions in the world. What a gift! Following tourist guidebooks at first, we went to art galleries, Sunday flea markets, anthropological museums, and elegant colonial era churches. Of the churches, none stood out for us like Santa Maria de

Tonantzintla in Puebla. Here the delightful color and design exuberance of the native artisans completely overwhelms the European baroque structure itself. Everywhere dark-haired baby angels greet the eye, as well as so many depictions of native plants and flowers that fill every space. It's a celebratory chorus to the fruitful world.

Later, I began taking classes. I visited art galleries and attended lectures. I bought art and history books. I got to know contemporary artists. I became an eager and probably tiresome tour guide to innocent relatives and wives of business associates visiting my husband.

Throughout this time, I was fortunate to have women friends who shared my passion for Mexican art and history. We began organizing little excursions with a guide. We climbed pyramids in jungles and sometimes half-crawled about inside them. We wandered in cavernous abandoned churches, and visited local artisans in their homes and studios. We traveled in vans, jeeps, even a small plane. We stayed in jungle lodges where tree frogs and howler monkeys camped outside, in converted convents and monasteries with peeling frescoes, in something like a Holiday Inn.

Then, after twenty years I moved away. On one of my trips back my daughter and I took a day trip to the little town of Metepec known for its clay sculptures and garden pots and ornaments. This little "Arca de Noe" caught my eye immediately, but acting with false economy, I didn't purchase it. A few months later, my daughter gave it to me for Christmas. I look at it and think of her loving intuition as I stood in the shop admiring the piece, and remembering the gift of my years in Mexico, the gift of rearing my children there, and the people who made me welcome in their country. And of the brilliant artistic wealth I found there. Could there be a more delightful world!!

St. Bart's Bonnett
Adrienne Ingram

This straw hat was made by a resident of St. Bart's (St. Barthelemy, a French-speaking Caribbean island of only 9.7 square miles). This island is known for beautiful white-sand beaches, sailboats and yachts, designer shops, as well as high-end restaurants and historical attractions … in other words, a playground for the rich and famous. However, this island means so much more to me because it is the birthplace of my maternal grandparents.

In 2007 my sister and I, along with our spouses, made a voyage to St. Bart's to track our heritage. We were able to meet our mother's cousins (twice removed), to obtain marriage certificates from the town hall and photos of our great, great grandparents from a woman who lives there and does ancestry of those on the island. We can trace one ancestor back to 1659 who was among the original settlers that survived the second attempt to populate St. Bart's and was not killed off by the savage natives.

Since the island was very poor (survival was simply eking out an existence by farming on the limited arable land), commerce was nil. Over the centuries the salt flats have been the island's almost only source of exports. After the introduction of a particular palm tree in 1890, the leaves were fashioned into mooring ropes as well as very delicate strands to be woven into hats and baskets.

This straw hat reminds me of the hardships and the tenacity of my ancestors to survive and thrive over the years. My sister's extensive work of our ancestry proves from where we have come and who we are today.

Western Union Love Story
Calvin W. Jayroe

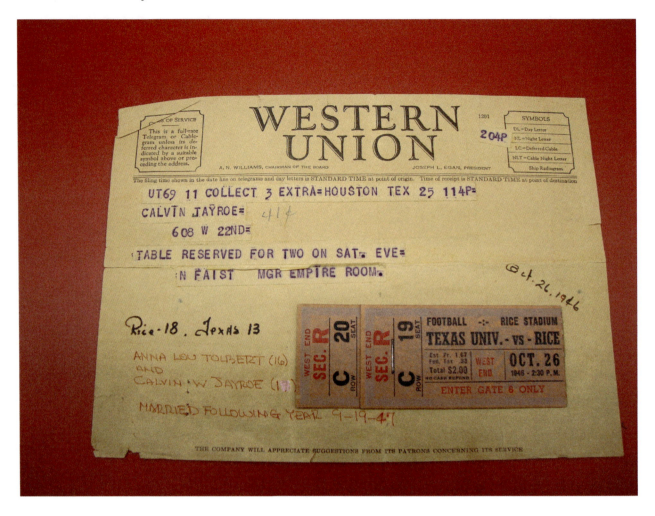

My keepsake tells a story about two kids that came together for a special occasion that became a love affair that has lasted over 73 years. I was a 17-year old freshman at The University of Texas and was smitten by a 16-year old girl named Anna who was a senior in high school. I was making frequent weekend trips to Lufkin, Texas to see her and wanted to do something to impress her. So, I invited her to go to the UT – Rice game on October 26, 1946 in Houston to be followed by dinner and dancing at the Rice Hotel Empire Room (a very special place in those days). Anna's parents gave permission as long as she spent the night at her aunt's house in Houston.

It was an exciting day for two youngsters in love. We had a wonderful time. A year later, we were married on September, 19, 1947. Upon graduation from high school, Anna enrolled at UT. We have had a wonderful life together. The football tickets are unique souvenirs but the telegram from Western Union is remarkable because it shows how special an event it was to have a reservation at the Empire Room of the historic Rice Hotel. In those days, the hotel confirmed your dinner reservation by sending you a telegram. Note that it cost 41 cents.

Longhorn Cap
Judy Johns

My husband, Jerry, was an avid University of Texas Longhorn fan. He bled burnt orange! Every year he had season tickets for the football and basketball games. And every year he bought a new Texas Logo cap to wear to the games.

At the start of the 2005 football season, he was very excited about the Longhorn's chances for winning the national championship in football. After the third game of the season, he started using a felt-tipped marker to place a tick mark after every win. As you can see there are 13 tick marks for 13 wins (an undefeated season).

The tick mark with a circle around it is the one for the national championship game when Texas beat the University of Southern California at the Rose Bowl. We weren't able to attend that game. We were in China, but we watched it on television in our hotel room. We celebrated the win in an English pub. We were probably the only Longhorn fans there.

Jerry never wore the cap again. It now belongs to my son, but the special memories it evokes belong to me.

Scud Missile Attack
Ellen Karas

My keepsake is a photograph of a SCUD missile attack in Riyadh, Saudi Arabia that occurred on February 24, 1991. In the photograph you see the SCUD blowing up after being intercepted by a Patriot missile. The small dotted line at the top left is the SCUD ablating (burning up from atmospheric friction). Thousands of this photograph were sold. My husband, Don Bomer, sold hundreds to friends, acquaintances, and the PX system. At the bottom left of this photograph, the photographer wrote "Don, this SCUD's for You."

2005 National Champions
Ed Keller

I'm a University of Texas fan; an Orange-Blood, a Hook-em Horns, Yea, Texas Fight, kind of guy. I go to all the football games and have since I graduated in 1962. So, of course, I went to the 2005 National Championship game where UT played the University of Southern California in the Rose Bowl. I not only went but collected memorabilia concerning that game. Some of my collection is pictured here, but I have newspapers, magazines, photos, videos, and other souvenirs related to the big game. In this picture are: Texas Monthly, Sports Illustrated, a Wheaties box (the breakfast of Champions), the ticket to the game, and a photo I snapped just as the game ended. This photo is a story unto itself. I think the scoreboard operator was so sure that USC was going to win that he typed up and displayed the scoreboard message, "University of Southern California BCS National Champions," before the game was over. I saw it and quickly took a picture of it. Thank goodness, I did because the message was immediately erased. Well, that's my story but I have one more thing to say: "HOOK-EM."

Dad's Mantel Clock
Pat Keller

This mantel clock was a wedding gift from Dad's co-workers. My parents were married in 1930 and the clock was on display in their house, on and off, for 78 years. Dad loved the clock and was very meticulous about keeping it wound and it kept perfect time. When they passed on, there was a lot of stuff to sort out. I selected the clock as something I wanted to have.

At my Dad's death, I took the clock and placed it on the mantel in my living room. Even though it eventually quit keeping good time, I've kept it as a small piece of my parents' history and a reminder of their long and happy marriage. It brings back pleasant memories.

My Bronze Shoes
Lou Kerby

Mother kept my little shoes in a chest for many years. She was a magazine reader and in one of the magazines, she saw an advertisement about electroplating baby shoes to preserve them and she sent my little pink sandals with hearts cut out of the leather to be bronzed as a gift for one of my birthdays. The bronzer also made bases for his products and would personalize them if requested. Mother requested that "Louise" be placed on the base. The short, slotted columns at the back were the picture frame, designed to hold a photo. A picture taken of me as the Roby mascot taken in 1934 or 1935, when I was three, was in the frame. The glass was broken years ago, but I still have the photo.

My husband, Ray, saw my bronzed shoes and took an interest in electroplating. Mother had also saved another pair of my shoes. They were white, high topped, two-buckle shoes. I was probably a year old when I wore them. Ray electroplated the pair, but one of them was lost in one of our moves. Ray also made the pedestal on which the shoe sits.

Latvian Lutheran Pastor's Cross
Paul Kronbergs

My keepsake is a silver Latvian Lutheran Pastor's cross. My father was a Latvian Lutheran Pastor, so were two of my uncles, my mother's father, one of her uncles, and both of her grandfathers. I was born in Latvia and so were all of my Latvian Lutheran Pastor relatives.

During World War II, I lost my father and my native land to the Russian communists. We escaped the Russian army by moving to Germany. After the war ended, we lived in DP (Displaced Persons) Camps for six years. The DP camps were supported and supplied by the United Nations Refugee Relief Organization. My mother's brother, Feliks, organized a Latvian Lutheran Congregation in our camp and served as its pastor. One of the other camp residents was a silver smith and an officer on the church council. He collected some Latvian silver coins from members of the congregation, melted them down, and created the silver cross and chain for my uncle Feliks.

A bachelor, Uncle Feliks decided to help my mother take care of and raise her three children. Through his connections, he found a sponsor for us that allowed us to come to the United States. Once in the USA, he and my mother continued to care for us until we were old enough to take care of ourselves. When Feliks died of cancer at the age of 55, I inherited his silver Latvian Lutheran Pastor's cross.

The Winner Gets the Last Laugh
Janet Lachman

In the fall of 1960, I was 19 years old and on my college debate team. Interestingly, the topic we debated that year was, RESOLVED: That the United States should adopt a program of compulsory health insurance for all citizens. La plus ça change, la plus ce même chose as they say. Anyway, it was a requirement that everyone on the debate team had to participate in several other events, one of which had to be solo. I don't remember if we picked one, or were assigned one – but I think it must have been assigned, because I ended up in the Humorous Toastmaster competition. We were expected to present a humorous speech that was thematic in nature, not a series of one-liners, and it had to be 5 to 7 minutes long.

I prepared my speech recounting what I thought was a humorous encounter with a horse, but when I did the first rehearsal for my fellow debate team members, their judgment was – Not funny. Needs a LOT of work. So, I went to the library and checked out a joke book, looked for jokes involving horses, and incorporated them into the speech. At the next rehearsal they said, "That's better," and thus encouraged, I checked out several more joke books and found jokes that weren't about horses that I could work into my story.

By the time of the competition, I was confident I wouldn't crash and burn, but I left nothing to chance. I delivered that speech in a slinky black dress, 4-inch strap heels, chandelier earrings and the most glamorous upsweep hairdo I could manage. Who knows what did it, but I brought down the house and won this first-place trophy.

That was 1960. You will notice that the statuette doesn't much resemble me, or a 19-year-old version of me in slinky dress, heels, earrings and upsweep. It does look exactly like what the competition organizers expected the winner to look like: a man in a buttoned-up, hideous early 1960's suit -- in other words, it looks like the guys that lost, not at all like the winner, ME. Even though it collects dust, and it's really ugly, and the pen probably stopped writing in 1961, I think I've kept it all these years because my feminist self has always loved the irony – a perfectly humorous prize for a humorous speech.

A Lasting Reminder of a Father's Love and Changing Times
Ben Lancashire

My father was born June 24, 1897 in the Upper Peninsula of Michigan in the town of Cheboygan which is right on Lake Michigan. His father (my grandfather) had emigrated from Portadown, Ireland where he had been a school teacher.

Grandfather had signed an indenture which required that he work as a lumber jack in a lumber camp near Cheboygan for one year in exchange for passage from Ireland to the United States. Cheboygan is where he met my grandmother. She had emigrated from England and they were married in Cheboygan where he worked in the lumber camp and they lived the rest of their lives.

They lived in a very small home without electricity for many years and I remember my father describing how he studied and did his homework using a kerosene lantern for light. After high school he was able to attend Michigan Agricultural College (now Michigan State University) by working on a Lake Michigan freighter in the summers and selling musical instruments and giving lessons to other college students during the school year. After graduate school he became a college professor teaching agronomy and horticulture and then later on went into business.

My mother and father raised my two brothers and me throughout the depression years. And this together with my father's humble beginnings in Cheboygan, Michigan created a home atmosphere of not only love but an appreciation for frugality and planning for the future. When I graduated from college in 1950, he gave me this 1923 silver dollar as a memento and reminder of the changing times. Included with the coin was the note on the right hand side of this page.

I have kept this coin and my father's note all these years not only as a reminder of the effect inflation has over many years but also as a reminder of what it was like to grow up with a loving father and mother. My wife, Sally and I have attempted to keep this flame glowing in our family as well.

To Ben,

The enclosed FRAGILE token is a lasting reminder of the changing times. When I was very young and full of misinformation, this token was used to pay a full-grown man for a ten- hour day's work at handling coal, lumber, bricks, or other objects.

Now that I am old, this token cannot be bought anywhere in the good old USA. This coin has been reduced from its former value to what a quarter used to buy. So, guard it carefully. You may never see its likes again.

Dad

The Family Bible
Sally Lancashire

The Bible shown on this page has been passed down in my family from generation to generation beginning in 1857. It has very special meaning as it brings closer and more real those family members who preceded me.

The Bible is quite large, measures approximately 12 by 18 inches, and is in remarkably good condition. There are a number of notations written on separate pages in the Bible that provide information dating back to 1832 with the birth of my great grandparents, Jane Steele McNaugher and Samuel McNaugher.

After marrying in 1857, they immigrated from the Protestant section of Northern Ireland, to Pittsburgh, Pennsylvania. My grandmother, mother, and I were all born in Pittsburgh.

This Bible has been in my possession since the death of my mother in 1964. With my advancing age, I just recently passed it on to my niece for safe-keeping. She will be the fifth generation of our family to possess it and hopefully, this chain will continue for many generations in the future.

Old Dependable
Clyde Lee

My father, Gabe Lee, gave this state-of-the-art electric fan to his new wife as a gift in 1928. It was a personal gift as well as a practical one as they were living on Heathman Plantation, an 8,000-acre cotton farming enterprise near Indianola, Mississippi. Electric power had recently been provided to the city of Indianola and to the plantation, but refrigerated air conditioning in homes and public buildings was a decade or more away. Thus, the new fan was a welcomed appliance in their home.

Even though it was minimally effective, our family appreciated having the electric fan to cool our home during those hot delta summers. In 1936, my father took a job working at a cottonseed oil mill in Indianola and moved the family "to town." The fan resided in our Indianola home until 1952, except for the four years my sister used it in her dormitory room at Millsaps College in Jackson, MS. She married an agricultural engineering graduate from Mississippi State College in 1952, and they took the fan to their centrally air-conditioned house. It was used occasionally, and my brother-in-law cleaned and lubricated it faithfully.

While the fan was in their custody, I earned a baccalaureate ('52) and a masters ('56) degree in civil engineering at Mississippi State and a doctoral degree in engineering at the University of California at Berkeley ('62). I also served two years on active duty in the U.S. Army (Artillery). I joined the faculty in the Department of Civil Engineering at The University of Texas at Austin in 1959 as an assistant professor.

In 1972, I married Mary McGraw Beard and that Christmas

my sister brought the fan from Yazoo City to Mary and me in Austin. When Mary's twin sister Martha visited us in Austin, she always wanted the fan blowing over her bed at night.

Mary and I sold our house in Austin and moved to Longhorn Village in August 2016. This meant considerable downsizing in the number of household items we could move. I'm glad that we decided to include our OLD DEPENDABLE fan in the move. It has prompted many fond memories, and we've turned it on several times to supplement the usually-adequate air conditioning system in our apartment. For me, it's a favorite keepsake.

Silver Baby Cup
Caroline LeGette

When I was born in 1951, I was given this silver baby cup. During this era, plastics and Tupperware were not readily available, so babies who graduated from bottle feeding were introduced to cups. I have always enjoyed this cup because it's a reminder of how things have changed during my life.

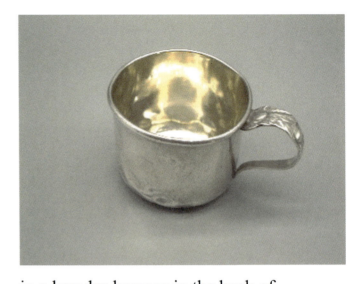

There are scratches, dings, and dents all over it, so I must have been a tough customer--- hard to please and always looking for more food and drink. I've kept the cup with me all these years because I can't imagine that anyone would want to take on something to polish.

It was a simpler time when I was born; for example, no air conditioning, no seat belts, no warnings about baby nutrition, etc. My parents drove from Kentucky to Florida one summer with me stowed in a laundry hamper in the back of their un-airconditioned little Jeep. After I cried long enough to fray their nerves, out of desperation, they stopped at a gas station for a cold Coca Cola. Once my bottle was filled with the Coke, I was a happy passenger. My parents always swore that this was my first soft drink, but it was certainly not my last. Sixty-eight years later, I still favor Coca Cola and I'm grateful that my teeth haven't fallen out.

Three Rings
Roberta Ling

Through my mother's side, we are a close-knit Scottish family who cherish our traditions and honor our ancestors. Because our family has been "top heavy" with boys, most of the "girlie" stuff has come down to me.

These rings are the wedding rings of the women who came before me. Each piece represents to me the hopes of a young bride and reflects the jewelry style of the era. The wide band of rose gold represents my great grandmother, a Victorian. The thin white band of platinum belonged to my grandmother, an Art Deco beauty. The twisted band of gold was made for my mother from an older family piece because money for jewelry was scarce during the Depression.

These three rings have been dear to my heart all my life. They are loving reminders of three women who have shaped who I am today.

Look What Clowning Around Got Me
Melva Martin

When I was a very young child I won this coin in a Halloween costume contest. It was held on the downtown streets of Olney, Texas. I was a clown chewing gum. The mask was bouncing around on my face. I must have been a funny sight. I am sure that is why I won.

The coin is a centennial half dollar. Remember the Alamo 1836 to 1936! I was born in 1936! My parents saved it for me. About 30 years ago I had it made into a pendant for a necklace!

My Family's Compact
Carol Maynier

My keepsake is a compact that has been passed down from my grandmother, to my mother, to me. The lid is a glass tile and the case is made of brass. It has faded a little over the years, but it is still beautiful to me. Unfortunately, I don't know much about it. My grandparents lived on a farm in Newcastle, Pennsylvania and while they were not poor, neither were they wealthy. I don't know where or how she got it, but this compact was probably a luxury for my grandmother. My mother inherited it from her and cherished it. She proudly displayed it on her dresser. And now, I have it as my keepsake.

Cremation Clock
Lynne Morgan

My keepsake is a Howard Miller wood clock. It is called a Continuum clock because it not only functions as a clock, but it also holds the remains of my late husband, David. It is a beautiful clock, keeps perfect time, and sits on my mantel above the fireplace. David was a collector and I have many things that he collected over the years. He especially loved clocks so it seemed like a perfect place to store his ashes. Whenever, I want to know the time, he tells me.

It also reminds me of my former home and culture. It is a wonderful keepsake.
Sany Abraham

I love that I can reach out and touch something used or admired by those who have gone before.
Kay Allison

My keepsake makes me smile and brings back memories of the great time we had.
Sharon Bishop

Wherever I travel, my keepsake and my Mother go with me.
Marc Bernat

Maybe it was destiny, I don't know, but you can see we were meant for each other.
Mac Booth

Having it in my home gives me pleasure daily. I want to pass it on to my children.
Pat Corlett

A Wonnerful-A Wonnerful Accordion
Deb Neth

Yep, that's me! And I am wearing the baggage that has accompanied my life's journey for almost 65 years—the adult sized Giulietti s32 model 41/120 18-pound handcrafted Italian accordion. I wonder if that is why I'm so short. . .

The now tarnished brass fittings on the exterior of its heavy-duty transport case, have carried dust all the way from my childhood home in St. Louis Park, Minnesota, to a practice cubical at the Accordiana Club and School in Minneapolis, to a downtown television station, to a Chicago touring engagement, and (less remarkably) to a Boston attic, a Sarasota storage space, a garage in Circle C Ranch, and finally to its current home here at Longhorn Village.

Mother was a music-loving Scandinavian and Dad was a 100% German American to whose ear the accordion sounded like home. My folks bought this one used, and even so, I can't imagine the sacrifices my parents had to make in order to be able to afford this instrument and all the lessons that followed for the eldest of their six children. The dress I am wearing in this publicity photo probably cost my Dad a week's pay. I regret all of the complaining that I did and wish now that I would have practiced harder, longer, and more diligently. Redemption, however, may be at hand: At age 69½ I am once again strapped into the Giulietti and taking lessons. But this time it is my valiant husband who has to endure all my mistakes as the "tip jar" grows fatter with every slip of the tongue as I try to coax the "wonnerful-a-wonnerful" Beer Barrel Polka from the bellows, buttons, and keys of my precious Giulietti. Thanks Mom and Dad. Although I never made it to the Lawrence Welk Show, I love you for giving me so many opportunities to flourish.

Baby Caps
Jenny Nimnicht

Long before I was born, mothers traditionally dressed their babies in baby caps after they were born and infants wore them for many months. My keepsakes are two baby caps that my Grandmother made for my mother; ones that I wore when I was a baby. My children also wore them. The caps are delicate, hand-sewn from fine batiste cotton and lace. They are beautifully detailed. The larger one has a pink ribbon running through it. The smaller one has a cream ribbon running around the front of the cap. They are well over 100 years old.

My grandparents emigrated from South Carolina to Oklahoma. It was called Indian Territory at the time and didn't become a state until 1907. My mother was born in 1902. I can envision my grandmother sitting by a fireplace with needle and thread carefully stitching these beautiful caps. It must have taken an incredible amount of time to create them. Boys and girls wore baby caps and boys even wore dresses when they were little. My how times have changed. Back then, whenever you took your baby out, you always made sure he or she had on a baby cap. It's different today. Most mothers are told that their baby doesn't need to wear a cap at all times unless it's cold.

I love these old caps. They remind me of my mother, grandmother, and brother who all wore them. They bring me joy when I see them. They will go to my daughter or the Bell County Texas Museum when I pass.

My Keepsakes
Margaret Osburn

In the fourth grade I moved from Memphis, Tennessee to a farm about 50 miles away. The four-room school house was about five miles from our house as the crow flies, but ten miles by school bus. Going and coming, the school bus lumbered over dusty gravel roads, stopping at almost every mail box or crossroad to pick up or let off students. The trip took about an hour each way. We passed the time by singing, telling jokes, playing tic-tac-toe, throwing spitballs, making friends (or enemies) and passing around autograph books, etc. The autograph books were filled with verses like:

> Long may you live
> Long may you tarry
> Love who you may
> But mind who you marry.
>
> Or
>
> I love you little
> I love you big
> I love you like a little pig.

At the close of the school day, girls were allowed to board the bus first. This resulted in the boys asking girls to save them a seat. They might have to stand for the first mile or so until some of the students reached their destination. If you saved a seat for a boy, he might reward you with some little thing he carved out of cedar or give you a hand full of marbles that he won at recess.

My keepsakes are 80 years old and consist of a few cedar carvings, a tiny dough board with rolling pin, a miniature guitar, and a five-inch-long dagger with Jesse's name on it. I also kept my marbles which in four years filled up a one-quart fruit jar. I still have my dog-eared autograph book minus its cover.

Jogging My Memory
Joan Simpson Parks

My keepsake is a memory of a race I ran in Florida. I will share it with you.

It is dark when we jump into our car and head 45 miles southwest down the Florida Keys to the city of Marathon. We are wearing shorts, skivvy tops, and old men's shirts.... we will toss these during the race. Lunch (for after the race) is safely stowed in a cooler. It is crowded when we arrive, but we find a place to park at Knights Key. We do some pre-race stretching, a bit of running, and hustle up to US 1 to find a starting place in the mass of humanity.

The race director hollers in his megaphone, "Runners! On your mark! Ready! Go!" We quickly move to the side facing the Florida Bay. It is humid and the sun has barely broken through. The view is spectacular! We quickly move to the bay side and start our uphill climb knowing that once we hit the peak, where the Top of the Hill Jazz Band is playing, it is all downhill from there. We see our competition and make a move to pass. My goal is to stay on my feet and to run as fast as I can. I see the finish line and pick up my pace. My time is called out, and I hear, "Good job! Nice run! You might be Third!"

We grab a bottle of water and one of orange juice and join the spectators to cheer on the rest of the runners. It takes some time after everyone is off the course before we get the results. I am so pleased to see that I finished 2nd for my age. (It will be seven years before I win my age category.)

I have wonderful memories of my races and my racing days. The photograph shows some of the medals and ribbons I won. Now, I still run but only for fun, or when I am chasing down a tennis ball.

China Basket
Kaye Patterson

A favorite Aunt used to baby-sit with me alone; my brothers were off doing boy things with my parents. Aunt Ruth lived in a duplex that had an elderly widow upstairs. I would make up chords and songs on my Aunt's piano. The widow, Mrs. Burgess, would hear me warbling and invite me up for a visit. I'd make up stories or dance for her, etc. to the delight of both of us.

Mrs. Burgess had a china cabinet full of unique and beautiful objects that fascinated me. When she passed away, she left a note in a china basket that was her parting gift to me.

This basket with the blue forget-me-nots held my wedding bouquet ivy which my mom made sure I had to grace our first home (half of a Quonset hut). As a Navy wife, we often moved. This china basket made eleven moves during our first eight years of marriage without being broken. It resides beside my bed table to this day.

The Bell
Randy Patterson

As an only child growing up in Philadelphia suburbs at the beginning of World War II, my parents were often worried about the usual childhood illnesses --- appendicitis, tonsillitis, and the feared and widespread polio. As a result, they were cautious whenever I developed symptoms of an illness. I thus spent time confined to bed, even though I wasn't always sick. This resulted in some pretty boring days. My mom didn't work outside our home, but kept pretty busy with household chores and tending her "sick" son.

My bedroom was upstairs in our small house, so she provided me a small bell to ring when I wanted her attention. Even though I have graduated to more modern devices, I have kept the bell as a reminder of those early times.

Her Name is ART
Carol Paul

My keepsake is named ART. She came into our family in September of 1901 as a wedding gift to my grandparents. My grandfather was a watchmaker and hand engraver and grandmother was an opera singer. I know nothing about ART other than she is made of some kind of metal and sits on a rosewood stand with her name, "ART" on it. She traveled with my grandparents from Chicago to Telluride, to Las Cruces, to Sacramento, and to Los Angeles, to the home where I lived and where my grandparents came to live when I was about 10 years old.

      She sat on top of a music cabinet by the front door so she was always there to greet you coming in or going out. When my parents passed on, she came to live with me in Hawaii and moved with me to Longhorn Village. She has attended many get-togethers over the years and was always given a prominent place in the activities. If she would ever put that brush to canvas, I am sure there would be beautiful scenes of love and friendship portrayed.

My Dolls
Janet Pusey

The dolls and bear in the bed were given to me at Christmas and on my birthday. I didn't play with dolls much because I grew up on a farm about eight miles from the nearest town and my nearest playmate was a boy cousin. The largest doll has on a dress that was actually mine when I was a baby.

The doll on the stand belonged to my mother. She was about eight years old and living in Brighton, Colorado. She liked to skip rope on the sidewalk. One day a neighbor lady told her that she knew a little girl who skipped rope, got appendicitis and died. She said if my mother would stop skipping rope, she would give her a doll. My mother treasured the doll and passed it on to me. My sister-in-law made the clothes for the doll.

Whistler Lithograph
Bill Rhue

This is a lithograph of an original etching by Whistler that belonged to my favorite uncle. Whistler and other artists used lithographs (a type of printing using water and oil-based chemicals) to bring their work to a wider public beyond visitors to museums and galleries.

My uncle was not an art collector and we don't know how or why he came to possess this. We don't know how many copies of this lithograph were made but a Fort Worth art museum director told me there is a declining number in existence today. This lithograph has some monetary value, but for me its value is a sentimental one. Following my uncle's death, his wife gave this to me as something he wanted me to have.

When I was about fourteen, my uncle took me to a rural area of the county where we lived and taught me to drive his stick shift Chevrolet. By age fifteen, I was an experienced driver on the two lane roads that were common in rural Virginia at that time.

My uncle sold apples on street corners during the depression. He became a loyal supporter and defender of President Roosevelt who he believed brought the country out of its economic doldrums. I vividly recall many heated "discussions" between my uncle and conservative family members who felt F.D.R. embodied everything they disliked. Those "discussions" probably caused me to have a life-long interest in politics and political leaders.

Double Diamond Drop
Ann Rowland

My keepsake is a necklace featuring beautiful twin diamonds. My treasure didn't begin as a necklace however. The story began with my grandmother who became a widow at a very young age. She had a gentleman admirer who gave her a pair of diamond earrings hoping to convince her to marry him. He died unexpectedly however, before she gave him an answer to his proposal. Luckily, Granny got to keep the diamond earrings!

After her death, the earrings passed down to my Mother, who had them made into a double diamond ring which she wore every day. When the ring was passed down to me, I couldn't wear it on my right hand because it was uncomfortable when I played tennis. The ring was stored in a lockbox for a number of years until my dear husband had the idea of having it made into a double diamond drop. Now, it is with me always.

I feel special to have a hundred-year old piece of jewelry that has been cherished by three generations of women in my family. It makes me happy to know that the tradition will continue when it goes to my daughter.

Axe Throwing Practice

Christening Gown and Boy's Toys
Suzanne Schlindwein

Choosing a keepsake for this book was difficult. I have many keepsakes but I have narrowed it down to two that I want to share. One is a christening gown that I made for my daughter Pam, and the other is a box of toys that belonged to my son, Alex.

In the fall of 1959, I was expecting my first child, Pam and I began making her christening gown. Using fine batiste cotton and lace, I hand stitched every part of the gown, and made the gown and a camisole. My mother made a matching cap. I don't know how long it took but it must have taken a lot of time. I can't believe that my fingers were that strong and dexterous.

I must have constructed the pieces well. Pam was christened at three months. Her brother, Alex, wore the gown two years later and then two nieces also wore the gown for their christening, and two great nieces also wore it. I am now waiting for new babies to wear it. It brings back fond memories

I have a box of things that belonged to my son, Alex. After he was finished playing with them, I put them in a box for safe-keeping. I just knew that I should hold on to them and that they would provide me with wonderful memories later in my life. They certainly have. I love to open the box, look inside, take out an item or two and remember him when he was playing with them. It is difficult to describe the pleasure I derive from remembering the things the children used, and played with, and how proud I was of them. These things bring back those favorite memories and special feelings.

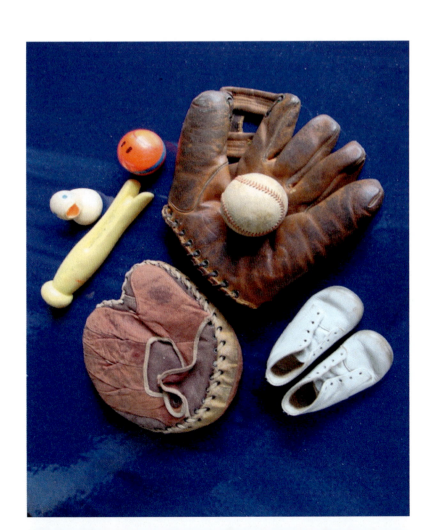

It was Meant to Be
Zel Schweitzer

My special keepsake is a painting I bought some years ago. I love the painting for its beauty and the interesting story that accompanies it.

Many years ago, my husband, Marty, and I lived in a resort community in Lake Arrowhead, California, near San Bernardino. Because of the lake, it was a tourist center with the typical tourist shops. One of the shops, an art store, had this beautiful painting of a view of the Mediterranean as seen from a room containing a small table by an open window. The table was set for dining for one and had a small vase with one flower sticking out of it. I could just feel the warm breeze coming off the sea. The painting was, for me, very expensive. I didn't want to pay the price and I didn't want to haggle with the owner over the cost.

I visited the shop frequently just to look at the painting. One day I went and it was gone. I was told a man bought it for his fiancée. I was heart-broken. On the occasions when I went back to the store and saw where the painting used to be I felt terrible; so sad. But one day, when I visited, it was back! The man and his fiancée broke up. She didn't want the painting. I guess it reminded her of him. I don't know.

Anyway, when I saw it, I was flabbergasted. I couldn't believe it! I was so happy! The shop owner said it was for sale at half-price. I immediately bought it and have had it for all these years. It has always been special to me. And guess what? On the back of the painting, is the title: "***It Was Meant To Be***." I know this painting was always meant to be my keepsake.

Silk Hose Eskimo Needlepoint
Beverly Shacklette

This needlepoint was purchased in the late 50's in Newfoundland, Canada. It was made by the First Nation people of the Greenfell Mission in Cornerbrook, Newfoundland, a town on the western coast of the island. At the time, my husband was in the Air Force and we lived in Stephenville, on a U.S. Air Force base.

The yarn used in this needlepoint piece is made from silk hose. The natives collected the hose, processed it, dyed it, and wove it into yarn which they used for stitching. I thought the process was unique and the piece was cute and caught my eye. I bought it and a couple of other craft pieces and kept them all these years.

I hope to pass these items on to my son who was born on the island in a military hospital at Ernest Harmon Air Force Base.

They remind me of a wonderful time in my life. They represent for me my happy childhood.
Judy Creveling

I treasure them and I treasure that wonderful, kind, thoughtful man.
Mary Jo Culver

Still a much loved treasure that stays nearby through a lifetime of good memories.
Jan Everett

That's my story. That's my keepsake.
Al Heilbrun

This is my most treasured physical memory, and it is an extra joy that it has so greatly outperformed its projected life.
Kurt Holleman

... a small piece of my parents' history and a reminder of their long and happy marriage.
Pat Keller

So Long, It's Been Good to Know Yuh
Ruth Shirley

When I was 8 years old, my family and I took our first airplane flight in Pampa, Texas. The plane was an open cockpit, two-seater and the pilot flew us individually. I was the last one to get a flight. Shortly after take-off, we saw this black wall of clouds. The pilot said, "We've got to get down," and he quickly landed the plane. We scurried home. It was Sunday, April 14, 1935; it was the day of the Great Dust Storm and the start of the Dust Bowl era. Many people thought it was the end of the world.

The photo you see is my keepsake of the event. I have had it all these years as a reminder of that time and all that happened. Woody Guthrie lived in Pampa in 1935 and wrote a song about the event. When we play this song in our Sip and Sing band, I always get out this photo and pass it around and tell the audience about the Dust Storm.

You probably have heard the song; "So Long, It's Been Good to Know Yuh. Here's a bit of the verse and chorus:

> Well the dust storm came, it came like thunder.
> It dusted us over, it dusted us under.
> It blocked all the traffic and blocked out the sun,
> And straightway for home all the people did run (singin')
>
> So long, it's been good to know yuh,
> So long, it's been good to know yuh,
> So long, it's been good to know yuh,
> But this dusty old dust is a-getting' my home
> And I've gotta be driftin' along.

The Little Kittens' Book
Connie Simpson

The Little Kittens' Nursery Rhymes was the first book I ever read. In fact, I learned to read as a result of this book. It started my life-long love for reading and cats. I have had this book for over seventy years. It is my keepsake.

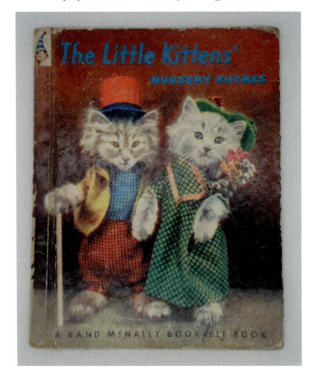

When I was just a toddler, my mother read this little book to me many times. As a result, I learned to recognize words, letters, and sounds. Soon, I could read it by myself. The nursery rhymes were fun to read and the photographs of the kittens were precious. All of the kittens were dressed in costumes associated with the rhymes. For example, the rhyme, "*Little Boy Blue Come Blow Your Horn,*" shows a little kitten with a golden horn fast-asleep against a bale of hay.

I guess reading about kittens imprinted on me the need to love and care for animals. My family and I lived on a four-acre spread on the edge of Dickinson, Texas and all kinds of stray animals came to us and we cared for them as our own. We felt it was our duty. When we sold the farm and moved to Longhorn Village, 5 cats and a dog moved with us. Along with the animals, my little Kittens' Book moved also.

My Dad Starts Painting After He Retires
Milt Simpson

My father, Benjamin Simpson, left me my keepsake; a painting he did after he retired. Dad was born in the town of Simyatich, Poland. One of the few family members to leave Eastern Europe, he arrived in New York city in the early twenties and went to work for an upholsterer in Brooklyn. Eventually, he opened his own upholstery business in Newark, New Jersey.

Although his work often required him to use stain, paint, and paint brushes, he didn't attempt painting on canvas until after he retired. His grand-daughter suggested painting as a means of dealing with his retirement and depression. Using my old oil paints, he first painted pictures of birds, clowns, and still lifes. In order to learn how to paint water and sky for future "sceneries," as he called them, he enrolled in an art class at Kean College in New Jersey. The class was a disappointment and he went back to painting on his own. He did his painting in the basement, producing 30 to 40 oil paintings before his death.

My keepsake is a painting he called, "Fantasy" which he completed in 1979. He was adamant that its frame be painted gold. This piece appeared in a book titled, "*A Time to Reap: Late Blooming Folk Artists*." I proudly hang it in my apartment and it reminds me of him.

My Dad, UT Golfer
Nancy Simpson

When I was growing up in Wichita Falls, Texas, I knew my Dad, Horace Downing, was a University of Texas fan. For several years, he and Mother and two other couples would go to a football game in Austin. When I was finishing high school, Daddy took out his UT Diploma, framed it, and hung it over his desk in our home. It was clear he wanted me to attend UT. So, I did. Almost forty years after my Dad began studying at UT, I began studying at UT. I graduated in 1967. Who could have guessed that in 2014 I would begin living in Longhorn Village!

Daddy attended Junior College, now Midwestern University, in Wichita Falls for two years and in 1927 enrolled in The University of Texas in Austin. He graduated with a degree in Business Administration on June 3, 1929. During his two years in Austin, Daddy played on the UT Men's Golf Team. As a kid, he caddied at Wichita Falls Country Club from about age 12 through high school. He knew - and loved - golf.

In 1926 men's golf was adopted by the Southwest Conference as an official sport. In 1927, golf was recognized as a varsity sport at UT. His coach was Tom Penick, older brother of legendary golf coach Harvey Penick.

Daddy was on the golf team for two years and lettered each year. He kept his letter sweater as a symbol of accomplishment and school pride.

Horace Downing's now 90-year old UT letterman's sweater is my keepsake.

A Marriage Proposal
Barbara Slaughter

My keepsake is a 57-year old three-page letter I received from my future husband, Dick, in which he proposed to me.

I was living in Roswell, New Mexico where I worked for Humble Oil (now Exxon) as the District Manager's Secretary. I met Dick at my church in February 1962 when he moved to Roswell to work for General Dynamics. He was an Engineer and worked on installing guidance systems for Atlas Missiles surrounding Walker Air Force Base, a Strategic Air Command base. It was during the Cold War and the government was installing these missiles aimed at Russia and Cuba.

In August, Dick took another job with North American Aviation in Tulsa, Oklahoma as an Engineer working on the Apollo Spacecraft project. He came to my house for dinner the night before he left for Tulsa and when he left he said, "Well, I might drop you a line when I get settled." That was it! After he had gone, I said, "Lord, I thought he was the one, but he is moving 600 miles away and if he is the one, you are going to have to do something because I've done all I can do."

Well, He did something!!! Dick told me later that the Lord really worked on him on his drive to Tulsa. He said he left Roswell at 5 a.m. and drove by my house before he left. Then he thought about me all way to Tulsa. Two weeks later I received this letter.

In the letter Dick asked to meet me at my mother's in Claude (near Amarillo), approximately halfway between Tulsa and Roswell. The last two paragraphs are very meaningful to me because of what they say. We met the weekend of the 8th and that was the weekend he proposed to me. I wasn't expecting it as I was dealing with a tumor which had just been discovered growing on my thyroid gland and I didn't know whether or not it was cancer. I was scheduled to have surgery the next Monday and I was uncertain as to how it was going to turn out. I told him I thought the answer was yes, but I asked him to wait until I got the results of the surgery to give him an answer. It was successful and the tumor was benign. Dick called me at the hospital that night and I said "Yes." I always jokingly told him I was under the influence of the anesthetic. We married in Roswell on February 23, 1963, had one son, Brooks Collier, and had 51+ wonderful years before Dick's death on September 23, 2014

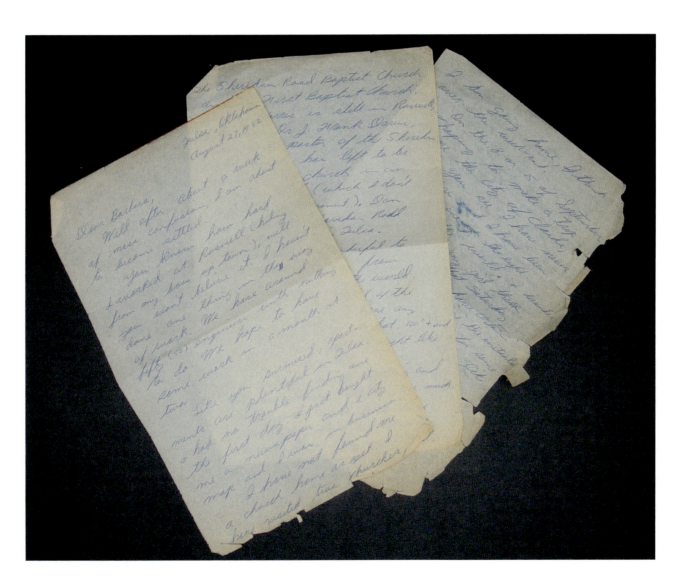

Mi Palabra
Louise Snell

A mere word, especially a word in Spanish, doesn't seem like something you'd regard as a precious keepsake, but in my case, that is exactly what it is. In the mid 1950's I was a college student in Madrid. One of my favorite courses was a class in philosophy taught by the eminent Spanish philosopher, Julian Marias. On the final exam I had to write an essay (in Spanish) concerning a philosophical concept we had studied in class.

Professor Marias gave me a good grade on my essay but he was much more interested in a word I had used: "futurizo." While it wasn't in the *Royal Spanish Dictionary of the Spanish Language* at the time, it seemed to him to perfectly describe the point I was trying to make in my essay. Although there are 10 other words relating to the word "future" in Spanish, the word "futurizo" has a meaning different from all the rest.

Many meetings, studies, and discussions are held at the Royal Academy to decide what new words will be accepted in each new edition of the official Spanish Language Dictionary. My word (roughly translated as "projected toward the future") finally made the cut in the 1993 edition. Thus, with Professor Marias as the driving force, "futurizo" is now a part of the Spanish language, a language spoken by more than 300 million people worldwide. Futurizo es mi palabra y mi keepsake preciosa.

My Mexican Knife
Tom Snell

I keep this little knife in a cup on my desk along with pencils, pens, and other things. I've had it since 1944 but I don't remember using it since it was given to me by my first girlfriend, Dulcie, a cute Latina who went to Junior High School with me in Oakland, California.

We really liked each other and she gave me the knife which she bought in Mexico and I gave her something in return, but I don't remember what it was. It must have made an impression on her because she said she still has it and keeps it in her jewelry chest.

Like many young romances we lost touch with other but reconnected recently. Somehow, she located me when I was 86 years old and wrote me to tell me she had cancer and was getting married. She was unsure about marrying and asked me if I thought it was the right thing to do at her age and with her condition.

Like most keepsakes, my knife is associated with memories about the person who gave it to me, what was happening at that time, and how life was so simple and easy. It reminds me that our lives can be complex and fraught with anxiety and yet full of happiness.

Portrait of Our Children
Shirley Steer

The unusually loud knock at my front door alerted me to hasten my steps to answer promptly. My husband, Bob, and I had just moved to Ganado, Texas, some 90 miles south of Houston. We had met only a few people so I was curious who might be at our door.

The woman at the door was unfamiliar. She introduced herself as Mrs. Strauss I invited her in and she immediately launched into her reason for seeking me out. She had heard that I played the piano (news travels fast in a small town) and her daughter's piano teacher had moved away. She pleaded with me to consider teaching her daughter, Sally.

I was intrigued by the request as doing so would create some extra income. I had previously taught piano and enjoyed it. However, I now had three children ages, 3, 4, and 7 and I didn't know how I could manage their care while teaching piano. I had wanted to have the children professionally photographed, but a limited budget did not provide for doing so. Perhaps teaching piano could make a photo possible.

I began a search for a baby-sitter and fortunately found a teen-ager looking for a means of making spending money. The sitter, Janie, was a precious, loving, attentive companion for my children. Very shortly I had enough students to make it possible for the professional photo to be taken. I was ecstatic. And now, the rest of the story.

Fifty years later, my son was passing through Wharton, Texas, the town in which the children's photo had been taken. He decided to stop for a cup of coffee and a kolache at a well-known bakery. Next door was the photographer's studio where my children's photo had been taken 50 years earlier. There, in the window, was the photo of the children on display. How delightful that the picture was valued by others as well as being my most treasured keepsake.

Silver Shoehorn
Phil Stevens

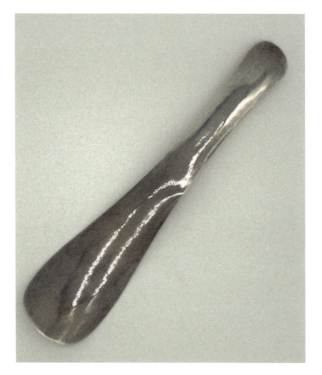

My keepsake is a silver shoehorn given to me by my mother before she died. It was made by Grandfather, Arthur Hartwell. Grandpa Hartwell was a silversmith in Gardner, Massachusetts who worked at the Arthur Stone Workshop from 1909 to 1937. This workshop became famous and pieces made there are in great demand from collectors and museums and are found in private collections. Silversmiths that worked for Stone "signed" their work. They had their initials stamped either under or after the "sterling" label of the crafted piece. In the case of my shoehorn, it is signed, "HARTWELL STERLING."

He was one of three silversmiths with their own shop. When I was a kid, I remember him working in his garage. I also remember him getting bars of silver for his inventory. Silver must have been a lot cheaper back then.

Most shoehorns today are made of plastic or some inexpensive type of metal. My shoehorn is unique because it is large (eight inches long) and is made of Sterling silver. It is probably a collector's piece, I don't know. But I do know that I cherish it because it was made by Grandfather and given to me by my mother.

Jackknife
Cliff Stripling

Like most boys in the rural town where I grew up, Jacksonville, Texas, I proudly owned a jackknife. I have lots of fond memories of time spent whittling various shapes and figures and cutting my fingers from time to time. It was not a gift; I bought it myself by saving my allowance until I had enough money, $5 or $6.00, I think; a lot of money for a nine or ten-year old boy at that time. That was a long time ago, but surprisingly it still looks almost brand new.

I used it mostly as a Boy Scout on camping expeditions, making snares, and other scouting activities. I always carried it with me until I went away to college. I also used it in games that boys our age played called "Mumbly-Peg."

Mumbly-Peg is a game of skill played with a jackknife. As I

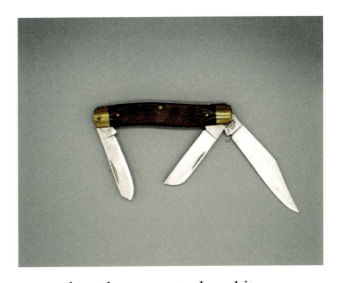

remember, the way we played it was to put a peg in the ground about 3 feet away from your foot. The object of the game was for your opponent to flip or toss the knife in a progression of moves such that, after each one, the knife sticks in the ground and stands erect between the peg and your foot. It got scary when the thrower got closer and closer to your foot. If the knife didn't stick, it was your turn and you tossed the knife at his foot. Lots of fun!

My Chocolate Set
Carolyn Ricks Stripling

This chocolate set with the markings "hand painted Nippon" has been in my family since my grandfather bought it for his mother in 1899 with the first money he made working in the family store in Plano, Texas. He was around ten years old at the time. My mother was given the set by her grandmother on my mom's tenth birthday.

Fast forward many years later and picture my mother bringing the set to me when she came to my fortieth birthday celebration. I had asked her to leave me the pitcher and cups when she made out her will. Being the sharp-witted person that she was, she appeared with the set and told me that items are labeled antiques when they are over forty. Since I should now be considered "over the hill" and entering the age of antiquity, she wanted to give me time to enjoy the set.

I kept mom's note to me that I found tucked in the pitcher. It says to love and enjoy the gift and pass it on to my daughter someday. Every time I pass by the chocolate set, I think of my mother. What a wonderful remembrance of a fantastic lady I called MOM.

Cypress Point Golf Cap
Harry Swanston

In the world of golf, few courses are as revered as the exclusive Cypress Point Club. It was created in 1928 by Alister Mackenzie, who in 1933 worked with Bobby Jones on the Augusta National Golf Club. Cypress Point is consistently rated in the top 3 courses ever created.

The course meanders through the coastal dunes of the Monterrey Peninsula in California, goes into forest on the front nine before re-emerging to the rocky coastline, for what many consider the best finishing holes in golf. The course will always have a place in the upper echelons of golf history.

It is virtually impossible to play the golf course unless invited by a member. In the mid 90's I was fortunate enough to be invited by a friend of mine, who knew a member, to play the course. The clubhouse and pro shop are pretty basic, but the handicap board listed names like Eastwood, Ueberroth and Costner. At that time, it cost $125 to play, much cheaper than the $320 at Pebble Beach, but we had to tee off before 7:30 AM and walk with caddies, so as not to interfere with member play. It would be difficult to interfere with member play since the average number of groups playing per day is 8!

After the round I purchased a Cypress Point cap, which to this day I have never worn outside, and that is my keepsake to serve as a memory of an unforgettable experience.

Four Generations of Sprunk Females
Pat Szmania

Shown in the photo are four generations of Sprunk women. It is 75 years old and was taken shortly after my sister's birth. From left to right are: my sister, Lee, my mother, me, my grandmother, and my great-grandmother. I am the only one now alive, so I treasure it as my keepsake.

My sister was a sickly child, stricken with Colic and needed a great deal of care. My grandmother and great-grandmother came to live with us to help with the nursing. I was about four years old at this time. Fortunately, my sister got well and went on to become a successful artist and business woman. She was fearless and tackled all types of projects.

My mother went to college and was one of the few women to work for Proctor and Gamble in their marketing department. She conducted research on product names and other marketing topics. She was a perfect mom and very involved in her community and was especially active in the League of Women Voters in Ohio.

My grandmother lived in Cincinnati, Ohio and I often spent summers with them. I loved it because I rode the train from our little town all the way down to Cincinnati. To this day, I still like to ride on trains. My grandmother was a good cook and loved having people over for dinner. My grandfather always cautioned people not to buy meat unless it came from his store.

My great-grandmother was very funny and had a great sense of humor. She was always telling jokes or funny stories. She always found something to say to make me laugh. She was a genuinely happy person. I remember she frequently used the phrase, "Dead game sport," which I learned meant someone who was plucky, brave, ready to respond to a challenge. To her, it was a good thing to be a "Dead game sport."

I feel so lucky to have this photo. It is a treasure for me to look at it and think about the wonderful women who meant so much to me. It is my very special keepsake.

Grandma Anderson's Trunk
Liz Tait

My keepsake story is about "Grandma Anderson's" trunk. My grandmother, Agda Eugenia Erickson brought it when she came to America in 1905 from Sweden.

The trunk is one of those old domed-top trunks with wooden slats and brass trim. Inside is a very heavy patchwork quilt that Agda made when she was a young wife. She went to northern Minnesota where she married my grandfather, John Frederick Anderson, who was 23 years older than she was! I think they must have been betrothed because I can't imagine putting your teenage daughter on a ship to a foreign country alone if they weren't!

The trunk was handed down to me by my father and it means a lot to me - it reminds me of the courage Agda must have had to get on that ship alone! I love to show it to others and tell them Agda's story. The address on the brass plate is "4122 Golfax Aw No, Minneapolis, Minn, USA", but in searching for that address I found that it must have been "4122 Colfax Ave No" which is a single-family home that was built in 1891 and is only a few blocks away from a Lutheran Church. Maybe a relative lived there??? Someday, there will probably be a fight for it between my four children! They all think it's really awesome!

161

Grandmother Williams and Comfort
Karen Teel

This small, leather-bound book entitled, **Comfort**, was given to my Grandmother Williams by a beloved friend and Princeton Seminary student, named Scott T. Brewer, in October, 1938, two months after my birth in August. His inscription spoke clearly to her: "May this little book help you to bring comfort to others."

My Grandmother Williams was **not** an ordinary woman - and she definitely was not an ordinary woman to many of the people who shared their lives with her in the small Oklahoma town of Wilburton many decades ago. She was often called upon when someone was sick or dying, and the family needed help.

Grandmother Williams gave the book to me in October, 1958, just before my graduation from Texas Tech University and prior to my acceptance into medical school at Baylor University. Inside the cover, she wrote: "Handed down to Karen from Grandmother Williams." I have treasured this book as a very special gift that had clear meaning to me.

One of the high points of both of our lives was the sharing of my graduation from Medical School in Houston. I was headed for a career practicing Pediatrics and she continued to care for others until she died at the age of 103. She sent me a clear message and prayer from **Comfort**:

> My portion of life, heavenly Father, with all its trials and sorrows, has been thy gift! How constant has been thy care, how faithful and uplifting thy Spirit's presence! Difficulties and sorrow have been met, but these have been passing clouds in a daytime of blessing. There is a balm that rises from the remembrances of the past which eases the ache in my heart for the faces I miss and challenges my heart to say: "What a privilege to have

lived and loved! The lines have fallen unto me in pleasant places. Father in heaven, receive my thanks, my praise, my love, for life which, sustaining hope unquenchable, inspires in me a faith unfailing. Amen.

How very fortunate we are when we are able to share our lives with family and friends who understand the blessing that their presence truly represents - when being there regularly reminds us of these gifts, when someone like Grandmother Williams is there, and we have the true essence of human life with us each and every day. Let us keep it near our hearts and never let it slip away.

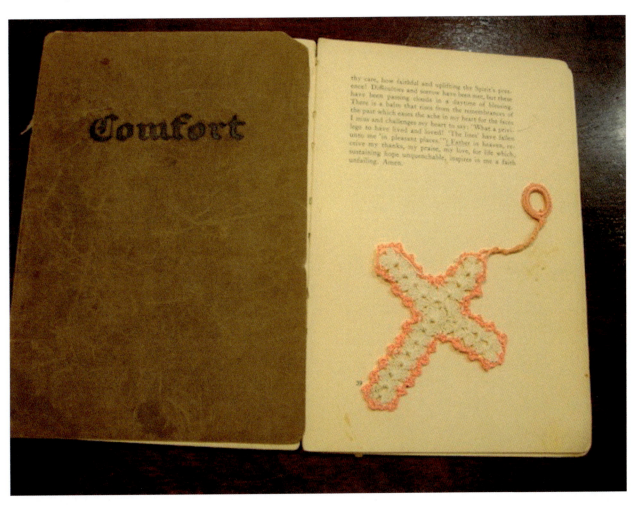

The Cordes Family
Warren Terry

My keepsake is an old photo of my Great-Grand Father, Heinrich (Henry) Cordes, and his family. A second-generation Texan, he met and married Anna Moellenberg who immigrated from Germany in 1896. They had a farm in Warrenton, Fayetteville County, Texas raising livestock and cotton. The photo taken around 1910 shows Henry and Anna, their five sons, Alfred, Harry, Lawrence, Weldon, and Heinrich Jr. in his mother's lap. The two girls were my grandmother, Leonora and Nellie.

Henry, a particularly gifted man, had a blacksmith shop, was the first in the area to have an indoor bathroom and electric lights powered by a generator long before rural electric co-ops came into existence. They also had a smoke house, butchering a hog on a regular basis.

As automobiles became fashionable in the cities, he purchased one only to find that it was a rare occasion when it could be used on the poor rural roads and he was a road commissioner elected to assist in correcting the problem. Unfortunately, with poor medical knowledge available, he died from prostate cancer at age 70. The burden of running the farm passed to his wife, Anna, and she carried out her duties with a Texas tough attitude. Even in her 80's, she could shoot as well as any man, run down a chicken and wring its neck, and make homemade bread daily.

Heinrich and Anna had seven children, the oldest daughter, my grandmother, Leonora, raised me. She never forgot her roots even after marrying the local school teacher, Benjamin Schulze, a physicist, who taught during the school year and many summers at the University of Oklahoma and the University of Texas. Such was the story of two farm kids, one with a seventh-grade education, the other a university scholar, but both country smart. The photo provides me with a graphic display of my ancestry and makes me proud knowing all they accomplished.

Life Magazine – The Texas Sniper
Ben Tobias

Like thousands of people everywhere, I will never forget where I was or what I was doing on August 1, 1966. My keepsake tells the story of what happened that day; that horrible day when Charles Whitman massacred his wife, mother, and 12 others and wounded 31 more. It was the most savaged one-man rampage in the history of American crime at the time.

I was the Hospital Administrator at Brackenridge Hospital, Austin's emergency receiving hospital. It was around 11:40 on a Monday morning and I was going over my time-sheets when I got a call from the emergency room supervisor that the hospital was receiving a lot of gun-shot victims. It was the start of a torturous day. We immediately enacted our emergency plan that we had rehearsed previously to handle such a situation. Thank goodness we did because there was so much to do and so many people to tend to. I will always be grateful to our employees and volunteers who came to our aid. So many people worked so hard to help us identify and treat people. One person I will never forget was Joe Roddy, a TV personality who helped us identify people. He stayed with us until early the next morning.

The Life magazine story about the massacre reminds me of that day and the tragedy. But I like to think about all the good people that did all they could to help.

Tatting
Phyllis Tobias

My keepsakes are a piece of tatted lace, a tatting shuttle, and sewing scissors. I don't know how old the tatted lace is. It was done by my mother and displayed on her buffet for many years. The shuttle, made of Bakelite, the first plastic made from synthetic components is at least 75 years old. The scissors are over 100 years old. My Grandmother and Mother were very strict about using the "sewing scissors." As the name implies, they were to be used only for sewing; never for cutting paper.

I don't know if tatting is popular anymore. It was when I was young. For those of you who are unfamiliar with it, let me provide a description.

Tatting is a technique for handcrafting a particularly durable lace from a series of knots and loops. Tatting can be used to make lace edging as well as doilies, collars, accessories such as earrings and necklaces, and other decorative pieces. The lace is formed by a pattern of rings and chains formed from a series of cow hitch or half-hitch knots, called double stitches, over a core thread. Gaps can be left between the stitches to form picots, which are used for practical construction as well as decorative effect.

These objects were passed down from mother to daughter. It was amazing how fast they could create the lace using the shuttle.

Johnny Appleseed
Polly Trusty

My keepsake is a Royal Doulton character mug. The character is Johnny Appleseed. My husband was in the military and he and our family lived in Germany when he was stationed there. Our kids were interested in the story of Johnny Appleseed when they were little. We acquired the mug in 1955. As a military family, we moved a lot and somehow it survived all the moves. Whenever we moved to a new home Johnny Appleseed was one of the first things that we unpacked so he could welcome us into our new home.

A Clovis Point
Robert L. Turner

Clovis points are fluted projectile points associated with the Clovis culture. They are chipped from jasper, chert, obsidian and other fine, brittle stone, and have a lance-shaped tip and very sharp edges.

Extending from the base toward the tip are shallow, concave grooves called "flutes" that may have helped the points be inserted into spear shafts. Typically, about four inches long and a third of an inch thick, they were sleek and often beautifully made. Dating back some 13,500 years, Clovis points are mostly found in North America. They get their name from the city of Clovis, New Mexico where examples were first found in 1929 at a mammoth kill site. Clovis points preceded the bow and arrow by 11,000 years in Texas.

This particular point was found in Camp County, Texas sometime in the 1930's. It is the oldest of a collection of 1,300 dart and spear points from Camp county. I have completed an analysis of this point collection and a report will be published soon.

As an avocational archeologist, I treasure this point as my keepsake. I have had it for 71 years. It will go to a Texas depository for archaeological materials when I pass on.

Jim Bowie's I.O.U.
Rip Van Winkle

I don't actually remember when, where, or how I got this relic, that I have carried around for years. As you can imagine, it is brittle and yellowed with age. Given Jim Bowie's reputation, I also can't imagine anyone loaning him any money, but that's another story. As you know, Bowie was famous for his knife, and for dying in the battle of the Alamo.

My House
Pam Vessels

In 1972 I was a young wife, new mother, and a nurse. Unfortunately, I had very little self-esteem. My voice was considered of no value. I wrote poetry but was convinced by my husband and family that my words were not worth anything. Their critiques hurt deeply.

One day, as I was walking through the living room, I heard a woman reading her award-winning poetry on the Phil Donahue show. Her poems were similar to mine. The poet was Nikki Giovanni and she was reading from her newest book, **My House**. I rushed out with my baby in my arms to buy her new book. It was the first time I knew that I really had a voice. I felt validated.

Since that day, that small book has travelled with me everywhere. Many years later, I met Ms. Giovanni and had her sign the book.

Words are powerful. They changed the course of my life. I am valuable and I have a voice. Thank you, Nikki.

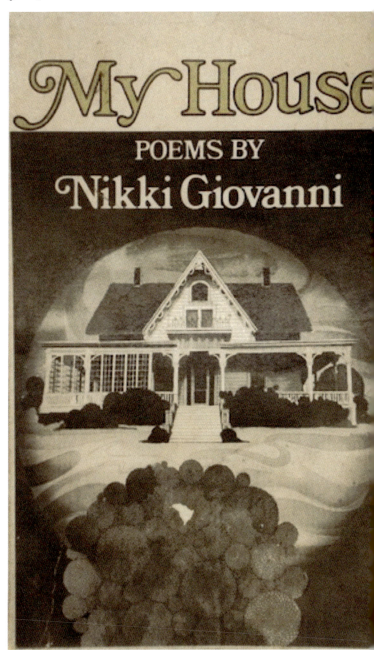

A Shiny Metal Object
Joe Wakefield

My keepsake is an award I won for winning a triathlon. Let me give you some background. After retiring from teaching, my wife Claudette joined a women's training group, appropriately named "Tough Cookies Don't Crumble." Initially, I was a cheerleader/photographer, but she was having so much fun that I wanted to participate too. We joined a mixed gender training group where the other participants and coaches were younger than our children. They were much faster than us yet very supportive. We trained with running, biking, swimming, and weight lifting 10 to 15 hours a week, then travelled to races together.

Fortunately, in triathlons the competition is flighted based on age (e.g., males, age 60-64). The older you get, the fewer people are crazy enough to race with you. So, when there's just a handful of competitors in your age group, you're more likely to win an award, referred to as "shiny metal objects." Claudette and I won several local races one year and qualified for the national championships held in Kansas City. The bad news is the race was called off because of thunderstorms. The good news is I could brag that "there I was with the best triathletes in the U.S. and not one of them finished ahead of me!"

My most dramatic race was the 2005 Iron Star half Ironman triathlon. It was my first race of that distance and I miscalculated the amount of water, electrolytes, and calories I would need for the 73.3-mile race. I became dehydrated and developed early heat exhaustion. I was fine on the swim, on the bike, and on the first part of the run. Half-way through the half-marathon run I began having leg cramps, then felt cold and clammy even though the temperature was around 90 degrees. I'm a physician and knew what was happening, but heck, I only had three miles to go! I walked/staggered across the finish line. Claudette took one look at me and led me to the medical tent. My blood pressure was 70 over 45. One hour and a liter of IV fluids later I was OK. Claudette and our kids grumbled at me for not stopping when my symptoms started but when I'd already raced for six hours, how could I give up? I did come in 13 minutes ahead of the second-place finisher in my age group. And that's how I got my shiny metal object.

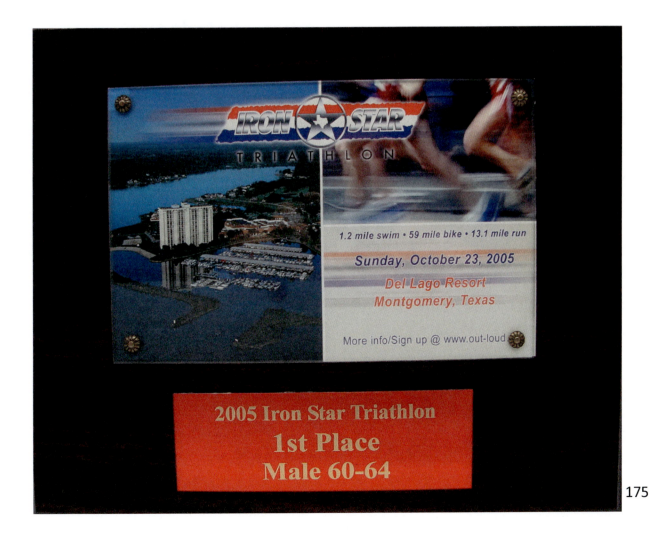

Mother's Silver Bell
Claudette Wakefield

I cannot remember a time when we didn't hear the sound of Mom's silver bell. It was always by my Mother's place at the dinner table. Being the youngest of three sisters, it was the signal and message for us to come peacefully and quietly (most of the time) to have lunch and dinner together as a family. This time was meant to teach and learn table manners and how to listen and take part in conversations with Mom and Dad, and also multiple guests that often shared our meals. During dinner, we were served several courses. Mother would ring the bell to alert the maids to change the dishes and bring the new course. This sounds very formal but it wasn't. After lunch and dinner, the maid would roll in the little trolley with coffee and pastries into the living room. We had extended family dinners weekly. The little silver bell was always there.

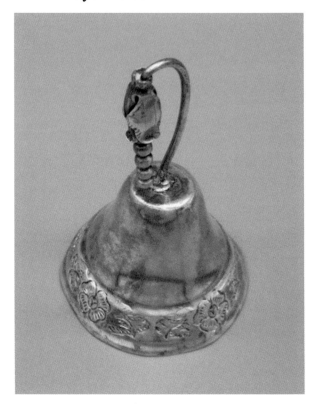

Oldsmobile Scramble Sweater
Pat Wendland

In another lifetime, somewhere in the early 1980's, the Oldsmobile car company sponsored golf tournaments throughout the United States called Oldsmobile Scrambles. Teams from throughout the U.S. competed first in a local tournament, then winners advanced to regional levels, ultimately to a national event.

Our winning team from Lakeway played next in San Antonio. Members of the winning team received a sweater which is my keepsake. I think the sweater is attractive, comfortable, and it reminds me of good friends, good times, and good golf.

A Cane-seated Rocking Chair
Bob Wetegrove

This rocking chair evokes strong feelings from me because it is a family heirloom going back to the days of the Civil War. One of my ancestors, Augustus Eldridge, was a corporal for three years in the 10th New York Volunteer Cavalry. He fought in frequent raids and was wounded in the battles of Chancellorsville and Gettysburg. After the war, he worked in the early days of the oil industry in Pennsylvania. He was a significant figure in the Eldridge family, which is the maternal side of my ancestry. The chair was given to him as a gift when he retired to farming.

The rocking chair is made of walnut, a dark, hard wood. It has been well cared for and I'm sure it has been re-caned many times over the decades of use. I sat on it many times as a child and an adult. The only restriction about sitting on it was not to have any sharp or bulky objects in one's trousers that might harm the cane seat.

I am happy that I am not the last living heir in the Eldridge line. I have a thirty-year-old Eldridge cousin who shows interest in family history. If I can foster this interest into a willingness to accept the cane-seated rocking chair when I pass on, I will have discharged an obligation.

Miss Kitty, My Siamese Cat
Peggy Wetegrove

When I lived in Chicago, over an 11-year period (1981-1992), I needed kidney dialysis and two kidney transplants. Two of my brothers each donated a kidney to me. My mother came to Chicago and took care of me during dialysis and during and after the transplants. At the time, we had two Siamese cats, and she especially loved the friendlier cat, Miss Kitty. She spent many hours with the cat on her lap, as she rocked in our rocking chair.

Many years later, my Mother was sick in a hospital in Houston. My Father had been dead for many years and she lived alone. We visited her in the hospital, and I found the perfect gift for her… a stuffed Siamese cat that looked just like Miss Kitty. She was thrilled when I presented it to her. After her recovery, she moved to an assisted living facility in Houston. This was 2007. Over the next four years, Mom endured many health crises, but she always assured me that Miss Kitty was her "security blanket," and she loved to rock her in her rocking chair. My Mom died in 2011, peacefully in her sleep. I inherited Miss Kitty and she still carries on as a wonderful reminder of my Mother's love and support.

Bone China Figurines
Juanita Williams

My husband bought a set of figurines for me in 1961. The set was comprised of 16 bone china figurines that were very old. They were made in France, Italy, and Germany. One has a date on it that says 1742. They are very delicate and the craftsmanship is incredible. The story of how we acquired them is interesting.

We used to go to estate sales in the Dallas area as a weekend activity. One lady had frequent sales and we often visited her. At one sale, I was particularly interested in some beautiful bed linens and wanted to buy them, but my husband saw these figurines and thought they were just beautiful. He offered the saleswoman $600 for the set. It was late in the day and I think she was tired and wanted to go home, so she took his offer. My husband called to me, "Juanita, can you write a check for $600?" I said, "No." My brother, who was with us, said, "Yes you can, Juanita. It's spelled S-i-x H-u-n-d-r-e-d D-o-l-l-a-r-s."

Index

Abraham,	Sany, 8-9, 107
Adams,	Glen, 10-11
Allison,	Kay, 12-13
Appleby,	Peggy, 14
Armitage,	Chuck, 15
Bartosh,	Sue, 16-17
Beckelhymer,	Eddy, 18
Befi,	Mary & Tony, 19
Behrhorst,	Wallace & Mary Louise, 20-21
Bernat,	Marc, 22
Bishop,	Sharon, 23
Bissett,	Jim, 24
Blauvelt,	Jim, 25
Bocek,	Edna, 26
Boldebuck,	James, 28-29, 131
Boldebuck,	Wanda, 30-31, 47
Booth,	Mac, 32-33
Brauss,	Orville, 34, 77, 107
Brustman,	Karen, 57
Carnes,	Bob, 35
Carnes,	Roberta, 36
Chambless,	Bill, 37
Colorito,	Sonia, 38
Cook,	Gareth & Janie, 40-41
Corlett,	Dick, 42
Corlett,	Pat, 43
Couch,	Norris, 44
Creveling,	Judy, 45
Culver,	Mary Jo, 46
Davies,	Morris, 48-49
Davis,	Anita, 50-51, 77
Davis,	Pat, 52
Dey,	Mische, 53
Dickson,	Dub, 54-55
Duke,	Connie, 107
Durso,	Sondra, 56
Ely,	Frank, 58-59
Ely,	Joan, 60-61
Evans,	Lois, 62
Evans,	Paul, 63
Everett,	Janet, 64
Fineg,	Jerry, 65
Freeman,	Bob, 66
Gallander,	Cathleen, 39
Gilliam,	Jim, 47, 57, 67, 107
Gilliam,	Judith, 68-69, 107
Hallenbeck,	Terri, 131
Harris,	Mary Juan, 70-71
Harris,	Teresa, 72-73
Heilbrun,	Al, 74-75
Heilbrun,	Marian, 76, 77, 107
Hein,	Peggy, 78-79
Henderson,	John & Charlotte, 80-81
Henegar,	Jim, 82
Hime,	Pat, 83
Holleman,	Curt, 84-85
Holleman,	Ruth, 86-87
Infante,	Judith, 88-89
Ingram,	Adrienne, 90-91, 107
Jayroe,	Calvin, 92-93
Johns,	Judy, 94
Karas,	Ellen, 95
Keller,	Ed, 96-97
Keller,	Pat, 98
Kerby,	Lou, 99
Kronbergs,	Paul, 100-101
Lachman,	Janet, 47, 102-103, 131
Lancashire,	Ben, 104-105
Lancashire,	Sally, 106
Lee,	Clyde, 108-109
LeGette,	Caroline, 110
Ling,	Roberta, 111
Lounsberry,	Joyce, 57

Martin,	Melva, 77, 112	Van Winkle,	Rip, 172
Maynier,	Carol, 113	Vessels,	Pam, 173
Miller,	Lloyd, 213	Wakefield,	Claudette, 47, 176
Morgan,	Lynne, 114	Wakefield,	Joe, 174-175
Neth,	Deb, 77, 116-117	Wendland,	Pat, 177
Nimnicht,	Jenny, 118-119	Wetegrove	Bob, 178-179
Osburn,	Margaret, 120-121	Wetegrove	Peggy, 180
Parks,	Joan, 122-123	Whitfield,	Roberta, 107
Patterson,	Kaye, 47, 124	Williams,	Juanita, 181
Patterson,	Randy, 47, 125	Yingling,	Ann, 107
Paul,	Carol, 126		
Payne,	Kathy, 107		
Pusey,	Janet, 107, 127		
Pusey,	Ken, 77, 107		
Robinson,	Corkey, 77, 107		
Rowland,	Ann, 77, 107, 130		
Rhue,	Bill, 128-129		
Schlindwein,	Suzanne, 132-133		
Schweitzer,	Zel, 134-135		
Shacklette,	Beverly, 136		
Shirley,	Ruth, 77, 107, 138-139		
Simpson,	Connie, 140		
Simpson,	Milt, 39, 57, 142-143		
Simpson,	Nancy, 144-145		
Slaughter,	Barbara, 146-147		
Snell,	Louise, 148		
Snell,	Tom, 149		
Stevens,	Phil, 47, 107, 131, 152		
Steer,	Shirley, 150-151		
Stripling,	Carolyn, 47, 154-155		
Stripling,	Cliff, 47, 107, 153		
Swanston,	Harry, 156-157		
Szmania,	Pat, 158-159		
Tait,	Liz, 160-161		
Teel,	Karen, 162-163		
Terry,	Warren, 164-165		
Tobias,	Ben, 166-167		
Tobias,	Phyllis, 168-169		
Trusty,	Polly, 170		
Turner,	Robert, 171		

Acknowledgments

Creating a book like this requires the help of many people. Obviously, the people who contributed their keepsakes and stories are paramount. Without their objects and personal memories, this book couldn't and wouldn't exist. To everyone, I offer my sincere thanks. You were fun to work with and are true treasures.

A huge thanks to Milt Simpson, my brilliant, creative, and sometimes exasperating friend who inspired me to do this project and was instrumental in the design of the book. His graphic design skills and attention to detail are exceptional and sincerely appreciated. I learned a lot from working with Milt and I will be forever thankful.

I am grateful to Judith Gilliam, Leslie Kjellstrand, and Michael Beebe for their editorial help. Thanks also, to Nicole Cochran for her able assistance with the copy machine. Thank you all.

About the Author

Jim Gilliam is a retired professor from The University of Texas at Austin, Special Education Department. Author of numerous books, journal articles, and psychological tests, he is best known for his work in the education of children with behavioral disorders, specifically children with Autism Spectrum Disorder. He has lectured and conducted clinics in the United States, Mexico, South America and Asia. His test, the ***Gilliam Autism Rating Scale*** is used throughout the world to identify children on the autism spectrum.

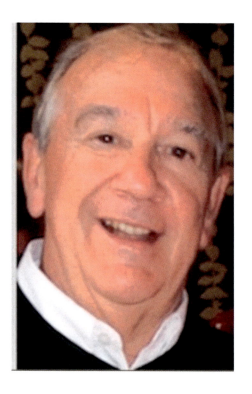

After retiring, he has pursued his interests in painting and music. His paintings of University of Texas Athletes are frequently on exhibition. He plays in the Sip & Sing band, and teaches a class on playing the ukulele at Longhorn Village.

Made in the USA
Coppell, TX
29 October 2019